G000015972

CONTENTS

BECOMING JOHN

Anorexia's Not Just For Girls

JOHN EVANS

ACKNOWLEDGEMENTS

To Mum, Dad and Angharad, thank you for standing by me when I tried to push you away. Your love and support has meant more to me than I have ever let on.

Thank you to Karen Law for encouraging me to do this and to Ros Draper for lending her excellent advice to a very inexperienced author.

To the immensely talented Helen Broadbridge (e-mail ogopogo@hotmail.co.uk), thank you for capturing my best side for the front cover. And thank you for being you, and for introducing me to the maddest dog in the world.

My appreciation to Sam Thomas and Nicholas Watts at www.mengetedstoo.co.uk, without your help and advice this book would never have seen the light of day.

To Ciaran Newell, Eve White and the wonderful, fantastic people at Kimmeridge Court, I owe you my life. Thank you for giving me the chance to become John again.

And to Hannah, Abbie, Margot and everyone who has shared this journey with me, your strength and compassion never ceases to astound me. Your names may have been changed but that doesn't alter the way I feel about each and every one of you. You've made me believe that this can be done.

FOREWORD

I am writing this foreword without having read John's book so I do not know what form the book has taken. I can just put together a few words expressing how this vicious, vile illness has affected John's life and of course ours—his parents and sister.

Where did it all begin? What could have turned our lovely, healthy boy—the child we hope would score a try for Wales, and who himself dreamt of playing for Everton—into a shuffling skeletal young man? Should we have been more aware of the early warning signs—the sit ups, press ups and obsessive running up and down stairs? Were we naive to believe that "he knew what he was doing" and "he was fine, don't worry" although he had started wearing baggy clothes and was looking very thin? Possibly, but it's an illness that we had no experience of and probably, like lots of people, thought it was an adolescent phase and that feeding him up would be the answer to the nightmare. Unfortunately this invidious complaint isn't so easily dealt with, neither is telling the victim—for that is what John was—not to be so stupid. He thought that if he was thin then he was fit, could run faster, score goals and win back the popularity he had had previously before the bullying began. It is only recently he has told us this.

We have cried seeing him fold his coat to sit on a hard chair, there being no flesh on him to sit comfortably, and when I had to put padding and bind his cracked, bleeding feet. The sight of our weak son having to lie on a special ripple mattress in hospital was really distressing. We were sad that we could not properly celebrate his 2:1 history degree, because he was disappointed with himself for not getting a first—another sign of this illness nothing except perfection is ever good enough.

Fortunately John received excellent support whilst at Leicester University and we thought he had beaten Anorexia, but it was to flare up again when he started work. The long early morning walks, cycle rides and weight lifting together with starvation type meals contributed to a recurrence of the eating disorder, although again John thought he was in control.

We shall forever be indebted to Kimmeridge Court for giving him such wonderful treatment, thank you for saving our son's life. We are pleased that John has at last overcome this hateful disorder and he is confident he will never again be under its control.

We are grateful to John's friends who have been so loyal to him and have shown him that there is life beyond Anorexia.

To John I say, you will always have the love and support of your family, we are so proud of you, you do now have control of your life—use it wisely.

But this is John's book, he must tell his own story. We are just so grateful that this lovely, polite, articulate healthy young man is here with us. We hope this book will offer help and encouragement to others who are afflicted by an eating disorder.

Love Mum

WHEN JOHN MET ANOREXIA

SCENE 1—On a bus into Leicester. John, an eighteen year old student is on the way into town to buy some bathroom scales. The conversation in his head begins again.

Internal Voice 1   OK, it's four o'clock, that's just enough time to buy the scales and walk back before tea. Better not have too much before circuit training, don't want to weigh myself down.

Internal Voice 2   *You could have walked here too, but instead you took the bus with all the other fat people.*

Internal Voice 1   I know, I know, but really it's getting on and I have to be back for tea. I've got to eat something; I promised Mum and Dad I would eat something. Anyway, once I've bought these scales I can weigh myself all the time and make sure my weight stays the same. That will stop them worrying and it'll prove to everyone else how thin and sorted I am.

Internal Voice 2   *You're meant to be a man. Do you reckon any of the other students have Mummy and Daddy interfering and looking after them? What does it matter if you lose a bit more weight? You need to—look at how much your fitness has gone down in just six weeks. That last bleep test was an embarrassment. The way you barely jumped that hurdle, they were all laughing at you, all of them. You have to do more.*

Internal Voice 1   I know, I know and I promise I will do some more exercises when I get back from training, but I don't think I should be losing any more weight, I don't think I should be less than 7 ½ stone. I don't care what my parents say, but maybe if I tell them I'm getting some scales and that I'm making sure I'm ok, then they'll leave me alone to get on with my exercise and have the children's portions. I'm still really tired—maybe I should go to the doctor just to get it checked, just make sure it's not meningitis. I do have a lot of the symptoms . . .

Internal Voice 2 *Meningitis! What, you some kind of medical genius now? You're not ill, you're just unfit. Get off at the next stop and walk the rest of the way. Doesn't matter if you're late for tea, food's rubbish anyway and you'll only make a fool of yourself chucking it all up after all the extra running you'll have to do tonight. Get off, get the scales, go straight to training and if you burn enough calories you can have some supper. That's the only way you'll get fit. You know what you're like, how fat and dislikeable you used to be. You're a walking doughnut. Do you remember when everyone used to call you that, "John the Doughnut", everyone laughing at your stupid, fat little body as you tried to keep up with them? And when did that change? Come on, admit it. The only time they stopped sneering at you, the only time they got anywhere near liking you, was when you were thin. That is the only thing people like about you.*

Internal Voice 1 Yeah I know, but Dad's been on and on at me to go to the doctor's about how tired I am. I can't keep falling asleep in lectures can I? If I don't get a first I'm going to be even more of a failure. Maybe if I go and get the all-clear he'll be happy. I can use the scales down the gym and then I'll get my own at the weekend, and I promise to walk there and back when I go. I know it'll be a waste of time but at least it will get Dad off my back. There has to be something wrong, else I would be feeling so much fitter after all this exercise, like I should be.

Internal Voice 2 *You have to do more, you idiot, especially you with your stupid, fat, doughnut of a body. I told you, you have to do more exercise than everyone else just to stay as thin and as fit as them, let alone go beyond that. Fine, go to the doctor if you like, but don't come crying to me when he has you lying down for hours, wasting all that time when you could be exercising. Meningitis! You really think a lot of* *yourself don't you? "Now you've found your friends for life, help save their life"? In case you hadn't noticed, you have no friends here, and no-one will like you UNLESS YOU ARE THIN! And you better get those scales, and you better weigh yourself after every meal and every run and every shower and first thing in the morning. It's the only way you can keep control.*

SCENE 2—The room above the Doctor's surgery. John has been taken here by the friendly nurse, who seemed quite concerned when he presented himself to her.

Internal Voice 1   Don't know why they've put me up here. All I said was that I'd been feeling a bit tired. She took one look at me and sent me straight to the nurse. Maybe I do look like I might have meningitis. Hope they don't keep me here for too long; need to get back to see the menu for tonight so I can prepare for the meal. Can't eat any later than six, won't leave enough time before training.

Internal Voice 2   *Idiot! Didn't I tell you this was a waste of time? You won't even get to see a Doctor stuck up here, they'll just fob you off with a nurse. You better not lie on that bed, though that's just the kind of pathetic thing you would do isn't it? See that magazine there, the one with the "Get a six-pack" guide. Pick it up, read it and absorb all the information you can before they stop you. You need all the help you can get because there is no way you will get muscles like that the way you are going. Look at those fitness regimes, that is what you have to do to make yourself ok; in fact you have to do even more than that, just to make yourself that bit better, just so no-one can say they are as good as you. Pick it up and walk around while reading, burn a few more calories. Never stand still, or they will all gang up on you like before— "lazy", "Penfold", "Doughnut" . . .*

SCENE 3—The Doctor's Room. John is sitting with the Doctor, half listening to what he is being told, half worried by having sat down for so long.

Internal Voice 1   All these questions, why all these questions about food and exercise and weight? What's that got to do with being tired? I've said that I'm trying to build my fitness up, that I haven't got that much time for sleep, but she keeps banging on about food. Can't believe my weight has gone down to six stone—didn't mean for that to happen. Still, no-one can say I'm fat now, can they, surely? No more Mr Average. They'll all be congratulating me on my willpower when I tell them about it. A real success story—"Slim line John" . . . .

God I'm tired, sitting down always makes me tired. Didn't think I'd be here this long. If I have anything much to eat when I get back I won't have any time to warm up before training. Can't get the bus back after all this sitting down . . .

What was that she said? Something about Anorexia? That's weird. That's that thing those stupid girls get, where they don't eat *anything*. Don't know why she's brought that up, I eat loads, too much really. Talking of which, probably no time to eat anything before training now. Ah well, I'll have an apple when I get back . . . .

What's she saying, drink a bit more water and get a blood test done? That all? Well that's easy enough, this Anorexia thing can't be all that serious. Yes, I suppose I could miss training tonight, if I go straight to bed and don't eat anything after I've walked home

John's Internal Voice   *Yes, that's what I'll do, just enough to make sure everyone can see how strong I am, just enough to stay in control. And if I am Anorexic, then no-one can expect me to eat at all, can they?*

TILL DEATH DO US PART

It is extremely difficult, if not impossible, to accurately describe what it is like to suffer from an eating disorder. No matter how many times I have detailed the fear and the guilt and the overwhelming mental and physical tiredness, I don't believe that any of my "normal" friends and family have ever really understood the never-ending conflict that I have faced for half my life. To have asked them to understand is too much to expect, of course, as their son/brother/friend seemed to be voluntarily wilting before their eyes, never able to halt the descent despite continued assurances that I was "really trying".

A very simplistic comparison would be to see the relationship between my Anorexia and I as having been like a marriage. There is no doubt I regarded it as a lifelong commitment, with no other alternative once my eating disorder became a factor in my life. "In sickness and in health"? Certainly, I never let any illness or injury, or any of the serious health problems brought about by my low weight deflect me from what I "had" to do each day to satisfy my Anorexia. Being run over didn't stop me from cycling home; the cuts on my feet were no deterrent to my daily walking schedule; collapsing on the way back from University caused but momentary alarm, quickly forgotten amidst the compulsion to exercise away that night's calories.

"For richer, for poorer"? My eating disorder has been a major factor in my inability to forge a career for myself, indeed to stay in any job for more than a couple of years, impossible as I have found it to leave my eating disorder at home. And why would I want to, because Anorexia's part in this "marriage" has been to furnish me with the self-confidence and pride that I failed to muster from any other aspect of my life. I never felt more high than when someone praised me for losing weight, never more convinced of my strength and willpower when I was the only one in the office not to take a piece of cake when it was passed round. Losing weight was my one real achievement, something that I could wear as a badge of honour to the world, and Anorexia offered me the chance to preserve that achievement

15

for ever. All I had to do was to protect it, to hold it close and stop anyone who may have come between us from pulling us apart. No matter the effect on my relationships, my health, my career, my only priority in life had to be, and was, my "marriage" to my Anorexia.

"Till death do us part"? To the extent that Anorexia is a life-threatening illness, that could certainly be the case. On the other side of the equation, I'm not sure that Anorexia itself can be killed. I think perhaps the best I can hope for is a divorce, where Anorexia is no longer part of my everyday life, but nevertheless remains on the periphery, a defining imprint on the person I will become. I don't foresee ever being "cured" of my Anorexia, not if that means returning to the person and the life I had before it ripped my world apart. Divorce is a definite possibility and that is what I continue to work on today, but first of all I had to decide to fight back.

One of the great ironies of my "marriage" to Anorexia is that it has prevented me forming any kind of proper relationship; indeed, from experiencing so many of the life events that a man of thirty years of age should have been exposed to. When my friends were out getting drunk and chasing girls I was at home, running up and down the stairs. When I deigned to join them and they went for a takeaway, I would politely decline all offers of a chip, pretending I wasn't hungry. And when I went to the gym, whilst other men would look at their reflections face-to-face, checking out their "Pecs" and biceps, I would always look side-on, just to check that the packet of crisps I had eaten earlier had not turned me into a blimp. To me, being a man with Anorexia has been less about being a *man* and more about being anorexic, and how that has defined me amongst other men.

Eating disorders are generally perceived as being a female issue, and I'm sure this makes some men reluctant to come forward and ask for help. All I can say is that as a man with an eating disorder, I have never felt disadvantaged as compared with the female sufferers I have encountered. This is certainly true of my two inpatient admissions, where if anything I found it easier to integrate myself and to remain above the inevitable tensions that such an environment engenders primarily because I was the only male on the ward. I have also never felt stigmatised for having a "female condition", though I admit to being frustrated over the female-centric nature of almost all literature and research on the condition.

To the extent that I had ever thought about it, I had always viewed eating disorders as being a female issue and I was completely taken aback when Anorexia blasted into my life. Until just before my diagnosis, I had no inclination that there was anything wrong, other than that my diet and exercise regime was not leading to the anticipated improvements in my fitness level. I certainly would never have thought of myself as the type of person who might have a mental illness. Although it got me precious little credit at school, I was an intelligent boy and some of the behaviours I have engaged in to feed my Anorexia have bordered on the ludicrous.

When I was diagnosed, I had no comprehension that virtually every action and decision I took from that point on would be governed by my desire to remain thin. Once Anorexia was out in the open, instead of trying to move away from the illness I became more and more entrenched in the behaviours that had driven me to the point of physical collapse. I became even more obsessed with calorie-counting and exercising "enough" and became increasingly protective of my eating disorder at the expense of all other relationships, especially with my family. Everyone else became a potential or very real enemy, all acting against me to make me fat and unacceptable again and, whilst I sometimes played along and always, always promised that I was trying "really hard", I always kept Anorexia closest of all.

Whenever anyone tried to talk me out of my Anorexia, be they therapists, friends, family or work colleagues, they would emphasise the material things that the illness was impacting on—my poor health, my inability to play sport, my inability to keep warm in the winter—all of which were legitimate arguments and reasons to fight back. The thing is, though, that you quickly learn to shape your life around your Anorexia, accepting the things you lose as the price for living the life you believe will make you happy and acceptable. I've never been ignorant of the compromised life I have led, but when you don't believe that there is any way things can be different, you give up fighting and try to live the life that Anorexia has constructed for you. And it's not the material things that hurt the most—like I say you adapt to those and learn to shut out the pain your illness is causing those close to you.

What really grinds you down is the stuff no-one else can see, the things that never leave you until you go to sleep at night and which then reappear as soon as you wake in the morning. The thoughts that Anorexia puts in your head get louder and louder until you do whatever it is that will satisfy the illness, be it exercise or putting food in the bin or deciding not to go out and expose yourself to a potentially risky social situation. And the thoughts stay away, maybe for five minutes, or even an hour, but soon they come back, and the more they are indulged and obeyed the louder and more frequent and more intense they become until almost nothing else seems to matter other than doing whatever you can to shut them up, even for a second. And all the time you can see the pain of those close to you and the damage you are doing to yourself and you become angrier and more despairing at your failure to resist, but still you don't feel angry enough to fight back, nor do you ever really hope to do so.

And then something changes and you do fight back. And the thoughts get even stronger, because Anorexia doesn't give up easily and doesn't want to lose any ground to your friends or your family or your happiness. But if you keep getting back up and acting against Anorexia, its call gets less frequent and quieter and, eventually, it gets weaker and, in the end, it will leave me alone. That's my dream now, not to be the thinnest boy in the class, but to live the life I deserve, in which Anorexia is a memory, not my master.

When I began writing this book I struggled to get in touch with my illness, floating as I was on a cloud of encouragement and good feeling from the staff and other patients during my second Kimmeridge Court admission. Since reading over it in the months since my discharge, I have found my Anorexia impacting much harder on my life on the "outside", where I do not have the constant companionship to counteract its call. I continue to fight, however, because I know now that I do not deserve this, any more than anyone touched by this horrific illness deserves any of the heartache that inevitably follows in its wake. And I know that I have it within me to beat this, however long it takes and however hard that battle becomes, because I continue to see the damage it does to people I love and it still makes me angry. This anger, however, is different: not directed at myself for being weak or for disappointing my family, but aimed squarely at my Anorexia, which for so long appeared to be my friend, protecting me from ridicule and from fatness, but in reality decimated my life to the extent that in truth I had no life.

And part of my fight is to share my story, not because it is special or unique but precisely because it is neither of these things. I am no different from thousands of other men with this illness, but our stories are never heard above the hubbub about Size Zero models and celebrities. And yet in a way I am unique, in that I have yet to meet anyone with my precise background, and by recognising my uniqueness I am again fighting back against an illness that has done so much to make me a shadow of a human being. I have taken the decision to own my Anorexia, to recognise that it was indeed the most important part of me and my personality and I hope my story can provide a glimpse of what it feels like to live your whole life in accordance with the voice in your head and the number on the scales.

For now I reject my Anorexia, a process I hope and believe will be accelerated by sharing it and my story with as many people as possible. The thought of putting my thoughts into some sort of coherent narrative only occurred to me about halfway through my second admission, and I hope that my later diary entries were not influenced by the possibility that they might be shared by other people. The diary is a mixture of the lows and the highs, with every small achievement often followed by fresh doubts and anxieties. I have included some of the text messages that I received during my admission, each one of which boosted my momentum and kept me going through the bad times. I also made note of any tiny thing that gave me a lift, whether it be talking to someone or playing a board game, because these type of things were not only what got me through the days but were a vital part in my realisation that there was more to life than how I looked and even how others perceived me.

I could have doubled the length of this book by detailing all the extremes of behaviour that Anorexia has driven me to, all the things I have sacrificed to be the best anorexic that I can be. Many events have merged into one big anorexic melange, the details subsumed in the hourly grind of *walk, stand, starve, exercise*. Also, I don't want this to be a self-help manual for committed anorexics, ever anxious as I was to push the boundaries of their illness as far as possible. For the same reason there are no pictures here of "Anorexic John", because this story is as much about moving on from that world as it is about describing how it was to exist within it.

Anorexia is dark and dangerous and leaves a shell of a human being in its wake, and that is something I can never afford to forget. Anorexia can't be overcome with a click of the fingers and you can't "decide" to give it up, but if you do a hundred little things which counteract what you have been led to believe about yourself and about your place in the world, you can start to fight back and loosen its grip on your soul.

N.B. Although the ultimate aim of treatment is to remove the focus on shape and weight, the programme at Kimmeridge Court is coordinated around each patient's progression up the BMI (Body Mass Index) scale, in which a BMI of between 20 and 25 is considered to be within the healthy range for an adult. I have given my own BMI readings within my diary, both to add context to the daily fluctuations in my mood but also, hopefully, to demonstrate that as I got closer to a healthy weight, my thinking got clearer and my belief in myself and in my ability to recover were enhanced as my physical health improved.

This book and the diary that forms a major part of it were written at various stages over the past 18 months, and there are intermittent references to a fourteen year—and fifteen year—battle with Anorexia. To avoid confusion, I believe Anorexia grabbed hold of me at 16, I was diagnosed at 18, admitted to hospital for the first time at 25 and for the second time at 30. I am now 31.

KIMMERIDGE COURT DIARY WEEK 1

Initial Goals for Admission

A. Weight restoration → BMI 18-20. John has been advised to reach BMI 20
B. Improve physical state through weight restoration.
C. Reduce exercise level.
D. Challenge thoughts about having to exercise to earn food.
E. Tolerate weight restoration.
F. Participate in group programme appropriate to his needs.
G. Increase variety of foods eaten.
H. Increase locations where food is eaten.
I. Stop calorie counting.

Medium Term Goals

J. John to identify strengths and skills to help with his recovery.
K. To become used to and comfortable with a healthy weight.
L. To practice to maintain weight/shape on discharge.
M. To review occupational options and decide on future work.
N. To review previous psychological work and identify new areas of work or work to revisit.
O. To consider factors contributing to relapse and ways of managing these.
P. Review support available to John.

Admission number two started much like my first experience of Kimmeridge Court: overwhelming tiredness, massive relief at being given permission to step off the treadmill of my life, soon to be replaced by the realisation of quite how hard this was going to be. The comfort of half portions were offset by the void of days structured solely around mealtimes and subsequent "peer support" sessions, with no chance of getting outside and stretching my legs. At the same time as coming to terms with my "failure", I had to adapt to living in a female environment again, trying to establish a niche for myself within the group, all of whom had their own battles to fight and all of whom would clearly see me as a fraud. There were a few familiar faces such as Brian, my co-worker, and Amber, my Key Nurse, seemed prepared to adapt the programme much more to my individual circumstances than had been the case before. Maybe things could be different this time.

Monday 14 December: Admission Day 1

I don't know what to expect this time. I think I'm ok with the idea of weight gain but it's been so long I don't even know how I'll react if I'm above 43kg tomorrow. Do I really believe that I can be 'better'? Am I right to raise Mum and Dad's hopes again? Is this just an excuse to get away from work? *No, I need this*, I need a break from my life. I've hit a rut and this is the only way I can get out. I do have to resist becoming too safe here—this is not real life—but there is so much goodwill, especially from the staff, it's hard not to feel almost at home here.

Tuesday 15 December: Day 2

BMI: 14.9

Weird dream last night in which my parents were crying a lot. It kills me to think of how much I've hurt them and lied to them, but then that just shows how powerful this illness is. Dad is 77, we haven't that much time left together and I've wasted so many years getting angry with him for caring. He doesn't deserve it and I will never get that time back. That is why this decade has to be different.

I was happy to see how low my weight was this morning. Maybe I've underestimated how hard this will be. My instinct is still fear over weight gain, and this seems like the biggest thing in the world.

Wednesday 16 December: Day 3.

Another day to test the resolve—the only way I can deal with these bad times is to use them as a spur to keep going forward. I've focused so much on the food/exercise element of the illness that I've disregarded the importance of the structure that it gave me. To go from such a regimented day to life defined solely by mealtimes has been the hardest part so far and I just feel like running for it at the moment.

Highlight of the day—achieving 'advanced child' level in the *Sun* word game—my life truly has reached a new low!

Thursday 17 December: Day 4

BMI: 15.1

REALLY strange day. 0.7kg gained in three days—first time in years that gaining weight has not sent my head into a tailspin. I never thought I'd actually want to eat more but that curry barely covered the plate. I think it's because the meals are the only structure I have, as well as the frustration I've felt being indoors all the time—I dare say this feeling won't last. At least wearing my trainers, jeans and contact lenses I'm hanging on to a tiny bit of self-respect—I'm determined not to just lie around. It is definitely the exercise that is the hardest part. I can cope (I think) with the food but it feels so unnatural not to be able to go for a walk or at least go outside.

There is a better life out there for me, but I have to grasp it. If I make that choice then the people are here to help but I have to discover what it is about me that has held me back and what it is about me that is more powerful than the illness. Unless I find that it will continue to rule over me and that would be such a waste—I do believe that. Phoned Hannah—reckon she could be quite important in this, but wary of bringing her too close.

Good stuff—Calvin Klein socks off the staff for Christmas; whipped *TVQuick* Sudoku and won Scrabble. Come on!

Friday 18 December: Day 5

Quite a big day. Cling to things like last night—presents like that are not given to people no-one cares about. Something about me makes me stand out here and it certainly isn't my weight. There is nothing wrong with being trim and fit but it doesn't have to rule your life. BELIEVE that and you can believe anything. From Monday I need to work hard to change my life, that is how important it is. Every time I ignore the voices it is one finger off its grip and it can be beaten, but only I can do it. At the moment it's all words.

Top thing today—getting outside and finding out I can go for a walk—I have to prove to Amber that she is right to trust me.

Saturday 19 December: Day 6

Another good day all round-out at last! The temptation was there to walk further but why risk anything at this stage? If I am to be here for two and a half months then that's a lot of time in which to worry and muck things up, so I'm not going to start stressing when things are ok. I can compartmentalise everything when I'm here—I'm here to put on weight and I must direct all my efforts towards that goal—but I'm still nowhere near being able to accept this on the 'outside'. The sense of guilt is huge—I can cope when things are taken out of my control in hospital but freak out when the same happens at home. There are so many questions that I have to find an answer to;

> ➢ Why do I hold so much store by my weight?
> ➢ Do I use my Anorexia as a barrier to relationships, social life, better career, risk taking?
> ➢ Can I continue in my job, or even living in Poole, with so many memories and temptations?

I don't feel fatter at the moment, so see what Monday brings. I have to convince myself that I am not special, I don't have to exercise more than anyone else and no-one will think ill of me if I recover.

Top thing today: getting out and being back within half an hour. KEEP IT UP!

Sunday 20 December: Day 7

Excellent news about my friend's mother who got the all clear from cancer.

It's strange how shocked I can still be at the consequences of this illness, even when it has been the cornerstone of my life for over twelve years. I caught sight of myself in a full-length mirror today and it surprised me in a way that I haven't experienced for a long while. When you are in an environment like this, where the one thing that you definitely don't stand out for is how you look, it's easy to forget the impact, especially physically, that it can have.

Much like my first admission, I have yet to break down in support, answering every question with a jaunty "I'm fine", which is true to how I feel but again could be misconstrued. At the moment I am focused on my goals and happy with the way I'm going and with how my head is. The pain will come and may come soon, but until then I don't want to exaggerate my problems. Truth is the last week has been a blessed relief and, while it's important that I understand that this is not real life, I am not going to plead misery when I have no complaints.

Highlight of the day: news about Mrs Munroe beating cancer.

Monday 21 December: Day 8

BMI: 15.2

Really weird day, with my emotions thrown from one extreme to the other. I really felt ready for my first food increase and what I had was not overwhelming, but something didn't feel right. There is a sense that I should be feeling worse, that somehow I'm not conforming to type if I don't collapse in an emotional heap. Most of the time I can rationalise this part of the treatment—the weight will pile on, so why fight it—but I feel an overwhelming desire to be weighed, to reassure myself that things are not careering out of control. Will I be able to resist this when at home with my parents? I really don't know.

Another 'looking better' comment today. Sometimes I think I disregard these too easily as being what people think I want to hear. For someone who spends their entire life fishing for compliments, I am extremely reluctant to accept them when they arrive.

Today's high points—Hannah's visit. Just stay focused. You have come through worse and it's not too late, you can turn this around. PMA (*Positive Mental Attitude*)!

Tuesday 22 December: Day 9

Another long day, and plenty of time to reflect on the upcoming Christmas break. It seemed such a good idea at the time to get Mum and Dad onto my turf, but now it feels as though there is even more responsibility on me to have a good time. With only two rooms to run to I'm really going to have to focus. Superficially there should be no difference from being on the unit. I know what I'm eating and I know the limits on my exercise, but there will be extra temptation and extra freedom. I've pushed for this break so that Mum and Dad could have the Christmas they want, but is it really what I need at this point? I'm at such an early stage in fighting this that I am vulnerable to any misplaced comment or tension around food. There is nothing I want more than an enjoyable Christmas, but I don't know if I'm capable of delivering.

Wednesday 23 December: Day 10

Took my first risk today, the first of many that I think may be necessary if I am to recover at last. I had been feeling hungry, and it felt ok to share it with the nurse. Almost straight away it was discussed and I was offered the chance to add a little extra to my diet. It's weird how things that seem impossible outside can seem completely possible when surrounded by caring people. See what tomorrow brings but having just had the extra, I don't feel too bad. PMA.

WHERE DID IT ALL GO WRONG?

In the brief moments of reflection which Anorexia has permitted, my thoughts have invariably ended up in the same old circles asking the same old questions:

Why am I like this?

Why has this happened to me?

How can I be so stupid, obsessing over every single calorie and every single second of exercise lost?

My descent into Anorexia wasn't driven with any specific purpose, some media-driven Adonis that it was my goal in life to emulate. It wasn't an act of punishment or a cry for help, and it's only in recent years that I have come to recognise the degree to which Anorexia gave me the sense of pride and control over my life that I could not find anywhere else. I wanted to be thin and I wanted my friends and my family and the people who had bullied me to acknowledge that I was thin, because without their approval I could never be certain of my success, and it was a guarantee of my acceptability that I craved more than anything. The images of extreme thinness and sculptured bodies did not fuel the fire of my Anorexia, but once I was truly in the grip of the illness every ripped muscle and every article on the dangers of obesity gave me justification in my own mind to maintain my relationship with the illness. On the rare occasions that the benefits of being anorexic lapsed from my mind, a "Fat is Bad" headline would soon get me back on the road to emaciation. I wanted a six-pack because society demanded that I have a six-pack.

Before Anorexia tore the heart out of my life, and before the bullying I experienced sent me looking for a route to acceptability, my childhood at home with my parents and my sister was genuinely happy and I was confident when among my friends and peers. Issues around eating were more to do with taste and appearance than any knowledge of what was good or bad for me. My refusal to eat school dinners led to a letter of concern being sent home to my parents and if I was ever given my sister's cheese and salad filled packed lunch by mistake it went straight in the bin (if I could get past the dinner ladies). I knew what I liked and definitely knew what I wouldn't like and I was quite prepared to miss out on parties and events if there was a danger I might have to eat anything "horrible". I was a very active child, spending hours on my own playing football or just generally running around, but still I was one of the fattest boys in my year. Again, though, I had no real concept of "fat" and "thin", and I was perfectly happy in my own skin, at least until my physical flaws began to be pointed out to me by my friends.

Primary school was a generally happy experience for me, though towards the end I was developing a very definite sense of not being "cool" and of my heavier weight not being a good thing. I went from being so chatty that I got moved away from my friends in class to being scared of going on theme park rides in case I cried or threw up, giving everyone another excuse to pick on me. The switch from generally happy to quietly sad was imperceptible, although certain incidents stand out as my confidence continued on its downwards slide.

When I was eight, my teacher asked me to write on the blackboard the names of anyone who talked when he was outside the classroom. As punishment, they would then be made to stay inside at break time. Having been brought up to do as I was told, I never questioned this instruction, and I was shaken (if it's possible for an eight year old to be shaken) by how instantly unpopular this made me amongst my classmates. There was nothing more severe than a bit of name calling at this point, but I had a very definite sense of suddenly not being acceptable, of having to do something extra to counteract my lack of cool and my fatness. Doubt had entered my life for the first time.

It wasn't that I began to question my belief system—my parents had brought me up to be polite and to try hard at school and this is what I continued to do. The only thing was that "doing the right thing" and being praised for it by my parents was no longer enough. "Doing the right thing" when my teacher asked me to write the names on the board had led to hostility and sadness and the first misgivings I had encountered about who I was and what type of person I was. My response was to shrink away from any situations in which there existed the potential for further teasing, like learning to swim or taking part in the school play, while simultaneously doing all I could to gain that extra reassurance from friends and teachers that what I thought and what my parents said was right was indeed ok. As time went on, however, and as the bullying became more intense, a self-critical voice within me became so loud that no reassurance could assuage the doubts.

From the moment my eating disorder was diagnosed, I focused all my attention upon it and became convinced that, if I could just beat Anorexia, all the other aspects of my life would fall magically back into place. As I take my first steps towards recovery, I am now starting to view Anorexia as more a symptom, albeit a massive, life-harming symptom, of a much larger obstacle, namely my chronic lack of self-confidence. And the more I reflect on this and the reasons for it, the more my focus returns to that time in my life when I was suddenly confronted by the hostility of a class of eight year olds, angry at me for doing what I had been told to do by our teacher. Indelible doubts over my acceptability took root, only sporadically alleviated by moments of praise and validation, and I began the still-present habit of being openly and deliberately self-critical in order to elicit compliments to the contrary. I'd gone from a popular, happy young boy to a swotty, fat goody-two-shoes, and I had no idea how to change the situation, at least until losing weight offered a way out.

Comprehensive school loomed on the horizon like an electric storm cloud, offering up images in my mind of a daily ritual of beatings and having my head flushed down the toilet. The bullying never did reach this level, but what did occur was far more insidious and, worse still, came from boys who had previously been really good mates. What started as a bit of name-calling and teasing about my weight eventually enveloped everything from my glasses to my boxer shorts to my supposed similarity to the school caretaker. Looking back perhaps I took it all too seriously but when you are in that situation and everyone around you on the school bus seems to be picking on you for an hour every day it is difficult not to feel scared and very, very isolated. I was only hit a few times but that was enough to make me fear every journey to and from school and saw me withdrawing into myself more and more in a vain attempt to make everything go away. Eventually they got bored and moved onto other targets and, almost despite myself, I did begin to make new friends, but a sense of unacceptability had been firmly planted. I didn't like myself, and I certainly didn't like my body which had made me such a target. I couldn't see anything in my life that could improve my situation. I was rubbish at sport, always the last to be picked and often subjected to a "Who can tackle

John the hardest?" competition. Girls pretty much ignored me, though I wouldn't have known what to say to them anyway! Nobody would have been able to help me, even if I had opened up, so what was the point in saying anything? Loneliness was becoming my best friend.

Again, one incident keeps coming back to me as the moment I decided that I had to change. Yet another conversation with my friends had descended into an argument about how much I looked like the School Caretaker. "I'm not as fat as him" was my rather desperate argument, to which the reply came back, "You're not exactly thin though, are you?" And that was it. Nothing more than seven words which kept coming back to me, dominating my thoughts until whatever vestige of self-acceptability I retained evaporated away. "You're not exactly thin though, are you?" Seven words that confirmed my inability to match up to everyone else, as I had been trying so desperately to do since the age of eight. I was miserable because I was different, and if everyone else was going to stay the same, therefore I had to change. I had to stop being fat.

My initial plan of action lay more with upping my exercise regime than controlling my diet, although chocolate bars and desserts soon became a once-weekly treat. I spent some of my grandmother's inheritance on a football shirt and a set of weights—thus mapping out the path my life would take for the next sixteen years in one shopping spree!

I recognise now that what I thought were sensible moves towards a healthier diet were in fact the first steps into my anorexic future, but the changes at this point were gradual and I was still being fed well enough for them not to have a significant impact on my weight. Again in hindsight, I can see the warning signs. I began feeling a strong sense of pride in abstaining whilst my friends handed round the sweets and remember feeling particularly angry when Walkers increased the size of their crisp packets. I was yet to start obsessively calorie counting, but those extra 50 calories a day seemed so important, so abhorrent, that from then on no crisps were bought without my strict supervision. It didn't help either that one of my mates was a human dustbin, who could eat anything and still remained as thin as a rake. I took this as further evidence of my own "otherness", and it added further justification to my intention to eat less and exercise even more.

Slightly embarrassing though it is to admit, my Dad was still making me a packed lunch when I was studying for my A-Levels. At some point two slices of bread had become three and, whilst I do not remember this causing me any particular distress, the number of crisps handed out to friends gradually increased to the point where I was urging them to eat them for me. Anxious as I was to use every possible chance to exercise, I was the only one still willing to play football in the rain at break times, and when this was not possible I began compensating by doing a few more runs up and down the staircase at home.

As my fitness improved and other people's reactions to me became more positive, I got a feeling of self-gratification greater than I had experienced before or since. This was one place where I had done my best, where everyone praised my willpower and my new-found, slimmer physique. No more jokes about 'Big Fat John' or 'Jonah the Whale' or 'Doughnut' but a new, confident, 'slim line John' as my football coach had described me in the end of year report. What a boost that had been, written confirmation of my success at something appreciated by my peers, not like exam passes and 'being a good boy'. I ignored the fact that he had hardly ever picked me in the team and held dear those words of praise about my weight, which by this stage was becoming a real badge of honour.

As I became thinner, the bullying tailed off and an indelible link was formed between my weight and my entire self-esteem structure. I suddenly felt more confident and acceptable and every jokey comment about my "anorexic" appearance just reinforced my determination to build upon my success. Truth is, the moment my friends began to lay off and the name calling became less of a problem, I merely replaced that bullying with another, far more damaging version in the form of Anorexia. And again, I felt utterly helpless when it came to fighting back against an opponent that had an even greater advantage over me in that, to a large extent, he was me. From the moment I began to take pride in my appearance, Anorexia put its hand firmly on my forehead, while I flayed my arms around rather pathetically trying, sometimes, to land a punch. It is only in the last year, starting with my second inpatient admission, that I have been able to land some of those punches and to recognise Anorexia as the biggest bully I have ever had to face, rather than the great friend that I had regarded it to be.

From being one of the fattest boys in my year, I was now one of the slimmest and the reaction I got from my friends was much more positive. Confidence was still definitely a real issue—I kept my driving lessons a secret from my friends, convinced as I was that they would appear at regular intervals along the route to laugh at me as I trundled past—but bit by bit I was beginning to dip my toe into my adolescence (even daring to drink alcohol expressly against my father's wishes). There was no doubt, though, that my weight and my football knowledge were the only areas of my life in which I felt truly confident.

Practical things, like driving, were outside my comfort zone, but academically I had always excelled. My GCSE and A-Level results never really gave me much satisfaction because I felt as if I was merely matching my family's expectations and I put a lot of pressure upon myself to not just do as well as I could but to do better than everyone else. I couldn't shake the initial inadequacy I felt when I found myself struggling in Comprehensive school, having always been near the top of the class before arriving there. In time I found my feet, but any sense of intellectual superiority I might once have had, and thus another pillar of my tenuous self-esteem, had been pretty much eroded.

So, with no real achievements with which to fight back the negativity, losing weight stood out as a proper triumph. Now, after proving my strength and my willpower, I knew I was a success, no matter how bad other aspects of my life appeared: I knew I was thin. Neat though it would be to divide my life into "health" and "Anorexia", I cannot pinpoint one moment when this confidence was no longer enough, when my weight became not a source of pride but an obsession. Over a couple of years my purpose went from being fit to being demonstrably the thinnest person in my world, and it just felt like the only truly important thing was to keep proving how thin I was. My fitness and my weight loss were noteworthy achievements, and to maintain that buzz I knew I would have to get even fitter and even more slimline.

My 'Golden Summer' of 1998 when the end of my A-Levels coincided with the football World Cup was, in truth, a daily repetition of cricket, tennis, football, cycling and dog walking. My eating disorder had by this point become firmly entrenched, prevented from bursting out in its full glory only by the continued consumption of my mother's cooking. A post-exam holiday in Magaluf was my first all-enveloping experience as an anorexic, providing me with complete freedom to skip meals and to exercise at will. Being almost teetotal at this point, I did not share in my room-mate's hangovers and was thus up and awake much earlier than everyone else. After a lie-in until after the breakfast kitchen had closed, I took the opportunity presented by virtual solitude to embark on long, solitary walks and to continue my exercise regime in our hotel room.

Over the week I lost half a stone in weight—I jumped on the scales as soon as I got back from the airport—the first time I had noticed such a significant decline. Perhaps this was the last chance I really had to deflect myself from the path that I was subsequently to take, but the thought of talking to my parents about it never even crossed my mind and, in truth, I had lost the war before I was aware of the enemy I was facing.

Losing weight as opposed to building up my fitness had not been part of the plan for a couple of years and I resolved to correct this as soon as possible, before quickly reverting to what had by now become a ritualistic pattern of exercise. This was maintained right up until I left for University, by which time my family were expressing concern about my health, especially as I had begun to ask for child portions when we went out for meals. As a result of their "interference" I became even more secretive, eating alone more often and tiptoeing to the scales so that the frequency of my weight checks would go undiscovered. Whilst I remained at home, being watched over by my parents, my Anorexia was restrained. University brought it bulldozing through our lives.

KIMMERIDGE COURT DIARY
WEEK 2

Christmas has always been a difficult time for me and my Anorexia, with the weeks beforehand focusing with increasing dread on the prospect of eating all day and being obliged to stay indoors with the family. Since I began working as a Healthcare Assistant and latterly as a retail operative, I had been able to use the excuse of having to work over the Christmas period to avoid spending the holiday with my family but, in what I felt was quite a major step, I had invited my parents down to stay with me this year. This was, of course, before I decided to return to Kimmeridge Court, but the staff were very accommodating in letting me home so soon after my admission. I was sure that everything would be ok as I was now under strict orders on what to eat and not to exercise and had no intention of defying these instructions. I was also sure that my parents would be really happy to see me so positive and having made the decision to go back. Unfortunately, that's not quite what happened . . .

Thursday 24 December: Day 11

BMI: 15.4

Well that was pretty awful. I genuinely thought they would be pleased that I had entered treatment again, especially as it was my decision, but they seem to regard it as a waste of time. Dad couldn't understand how I'd gone backwards having been 'cured' the first time, while Mum reeled off a huge list of people who had been bullied but turned out ok. I know I told her in advance that I wouldn't be eating the same as them but that also seemed to come as a surprise. Perhaps I shouldn't have said anything about leaving Poole and my job, but I just want to be clear about where my head is at. Part of me does want to stay, but can I make a go of it here with so many bad memories stalking my every move? I don't know—I don't feel great pissing work around, even after last year, but I can't jeopardise any chance of recovery that I have, and I believe I can do it, even if no-one else does.

They still can't grasp that it's a mental illness, that it controls my mood and my actions and that I want nothing more but to end this and to banish it from my life. When Mum had a go at me for living in a tip, I wanted to explain that I hadn't had the time to tidy up due to my restrictive life structure and all the exercise I "have" to do—I know they're tired of hearing it and to be honest I'm tired of trying to explain that this is not some intentional, attention-seeking game I'm playing, it's my life and it's crap. There probably is some truth in her saying that I haven't grown up since I was twelve, but I would counter that by saying that as I haven't been happy since then it's no surprise that I want to cling onto aspects of that time. I do understand why they're sceptical, why they think I don't stick anything and why they need proof, and to be honest I wouldn't blame them if they walked away. But when Mum looked at me like I was an idiot for suggesting that staying four years out of Kimmeridge Court was actually something of a success in the context of eating disorders then I guess it summed up exactly how far I have got to go here. The only thing I can do is try to prove them wrong and this has only strengthened my resolve. I still have time to be the son they always wanted me to be and whether they believe me or not, that remains a huge motivation. But most of all I want this for myself, so that I can enjoy the life I have before me, not regret the one I'm leaving behind. I know I have so much to live for and if I have to prove myself to my parents then hell, that's just one more hurdle to overcome.

Best thing of the day: finding out my mate is to become a father: there is a better life out there.

Friday 25 December: Day 12

Given everything that happened yesterday, today's gone about as well as I could have hoped—no fights, no arguments about food or exercise and I have felt ok eating two meals in front of my parents. Even so, definitely the toughest day of this admission. Still plenty of opportunities to give in to my Anorexia—some taken, some not—and it felt quite uncomfortable when we went out for a walk. The desire to go quicker, further, to climb steps and retrace old paths was very strong and again I was only partially resistant to the voice in my head. This is the best Christmas I've had with Mum and Dad in years, but there is no doubt that things are harder away from the support of Kimmeridge Court—I really feel the need to be there at the moment. Seeing my leg in the bath tonight it looked bigger, and I know this is the type of thing I am going to have to fight. Can't give up yet.

Good stuff: reminder that I have loads of friends and, hey, it's Christmas!

Sunday 27 December: Day 14

In some ways two weeks has flown by and yet the pre-Christmas world of work, the freezing cold and fretting about putting on weight seems a lifetime away. Truth is this is not going to be a twelve week job—I need ongoing monitoring and support and help to work out the proper food/exercise balance. How, for instance, do I live without calorie-counting in some way? How do I resist the lure of the scales? I managed this weekend, but what I can currently write off as being out of my control will not remain so for ever. One day, and then the rest of my life, I need to stand on my own two feet, make my own decisions, and that is why I need to *focus* now.

Good stuff: three ginger nuts, no arguments with my parents. PMA.

Monday 28 December: Day 15

BMI: 15.7

Today I again put on 0.6kg, despite my weekend at home. I remain focused enough to regard this as a positive, but I'm beginning to see/imagine physical changes and this was always going to be the test. If my anorexic voice is not to dominate, I need to use the support available, to allow other voices into my head as I try to resolve my issues with my weight. Above all, I need to look forward. It kills me to think of the pain caused, the opportunities lost and the damage done, but that is the point—it's done. I can't do anything about the past and the only way to partly correct previous mistakes is to fight to ensure that the future is free of this crap. PMA.

Good stuff: parents left on a good note—all I can ask.

Tuesday 29 December: Day 16

Feeling a bit anxious after snack out, not really because of what I had—which was ok—but because it was something I chose and which had more calories. I need to re-educate myself into looking on food as a pleasure, and maybe I need 'snack out' every week from now on. This feeling will pass if I maintain my focus and don't keep looking back. What's the point of taking the bad view of everything when you can look on the bright side of life? Life is definitely too short for this. If I back down at the first hurdle, if I never take the risk of seeing whether I can be different, then I am not the man I thought I was.

Wednesday 30 December: Day 17

I like to look upon today as being of some significance. Yesterday was all 'wrong'—eating loads, loss of control, no exercise to compensate = indigestion and feeling fat and less bony as my clothes seemed to cling to me so tightly. BUT this morning I look horrible, emaciated, *anorexic*. I am starting to see what others see, not all the time, but occasionally I get a different, non-anorexic perspective on my body which makes me realise how far I have to go. Everything I have ever believed is being challenged and if I keep going, keep taking risks and trusting what I am being told then things will change for the better.

For evening meal, a member of staff had some coleslaw on the table, and I ASKED if I could have some. Extra food! Unbelievable!

Why did I take the coleslaw? Why did I go beyond everything I've lived by for the past twelve years? Maybe because it is becoming more and more apparent how crap those twelve years have been. I need a new set of rules to live by and anything I can do to challenge my old beliefs, to take the risk that I never have before, I've got to do if I am to have a chance of a new life. It would be the easiest thing in the world to be here for two months, get up to BMI 20, and then go back to my old life, but I have a chance to be someone better, and last night and what Carol (*HCA who said I looked really handsome when I left at the end of my first admission*) said today has surely got to be positive motivation. If I don't take this chance then I really am an idiot.

I guess it's all about freedom. Freedom from the thoughts, to make my own decisions, to choose what I want, to do what I want, to be the person

I can be. As usual, last time I ran away and didn't confront it. Unless I face my fear head on, I will never have freedom.

Thursday 31 December: Day 18

BMI: 15.8

> *Hope I can support you through as you have through my hard times. I know the months ahead will be tough for you but I think they really will lead to a positive future. You have a lot to offer the world around you so don't give up on the fight you have at present.*
>
> *Hannah*

UNIVERSITY CHALLENGED

I had never really looked forward to going to University, or seen it as a great opportunity to meet new people or to 'discover myself'. I had no doubt that I would get a degree and University to me was just a means to an end. The only thing I was certain of was that I had to get away from home, far enough away so that I wouldn't be tempted to come home at weekends or to run back to Mummy at the first sign of difficulty. The thought of having more control over what I ate and did excited me; the fear of being isolated and picked on remained.

By lucky coincidence, one of my best friends from school had also been accepted by the University of Leicester, and I had confident visions of the two of us spending endless nights and weekends together going down the pub, watching football and reminiscing about the good/bad old days. He was in a separate Halls of Residence on the opposite side of the road, but it never occurred to me that he would make his own friends over there. Consequently, I made little or no attempt to ingratiate myself with anyone in my Halls, politely declining all offers to go out and "get off my face"—all those empty calories! Instead, I spent my evenings watching TV on my own, occasionally attempting to get my head round the French Wars of Religion or The Corn Laws and, increasingly, using the floor in my bedroom as a place to exercise after the University fitness centre closed at 9p.m. I didn't want to live the 'student experience' and assumed that I would get to know people through sport and by improving my fitness. As it turned out, the best friend I made in the first year was the manager of the fitness centre.

University was initially the worst, and then the best thing to happen to me as "Anorexic John", finally bringing it out into the open but then furnishing it with the ideal circumstances in which to thrive. I wasn't so much homesick as stuck in a kind of limbo—happy to be away from home but not yet ready to be an adult and to grasp the opportunities in life that my new-found independence offered up to me. I remained convinced of my essential self-worthlessness and in constant fear that I was one incident away from the ridicule and opprobrium of my fellow "Freshers". As they hadn't seen my formerly fat self I couldn't show them how brilliantly I had done to lose weight. I had to be seen as the best at something, as I had been in school in terms of knowing about football and being able to reel off the names of all 92 League grounds. Aware that this would be of no use to me in the adult world and even more convinced that academically I was now very much an also-ran, my weight seemed even more obviously to be my only cast-iron redeeming feature.

To stand out from the crowd and to prove my worth I felt I would have to get fitter again and so, armed with a £25 year-round pass to the University sports facilities, I began an excessive regime of football, tennis, circuit training, walking, gym work and climbing the fifteen flights of stairs to the History Department on an almost daily basis. Two meals a day were served at the Halls of Residence and, though I did not have complete control over the amount I was given, my routine request for 'small portions, please' seemed to become a subject of some amusement for the kitchen staff. Every spare second that was not taken up by eating, sleeping and studying was spent in pursuit of the superior level of fitness that I was convinced was the key to my happiness. My physical performance began to decline as exhaustion took hold, but this merely made me even more convinced of my lack of fitness and thus I pushed my body even harder.

Eventually, I had to accept the inevitable and went to the University health centre to try and find out why I was feeling so tired. The answer arrived when I stepped on the scales. I had lost one and a half stone in a little over six weeks and blood tests later revealed that many of my internal organs were on the brink of implosion. At the time I struggled to grasp what I was being told or the true gravity of my situation. Anorexia had not remotely crossed my mind as a possibility for me and I had no answers to all the questions that I was being bombarded with by my family. Truth be told as soon as Anorexia became part of the conversation I blocked out the rest of what was being said. There is no doubt that I took some sort of perverse pride in talking about how close I had come to really serious physical damage. Wasn't I dull, sensible John, who had never taken a risk in his whole life? Well look at me now, world, pushing my body up to and beyond its limits, how's that for being hard!?!

The diagnosis had remarkably little effect on my emotional state beyond filling me with an immense sense of relief—I finally had a reason for the physical decline I had experienced; I wasn't unfit, I was properly, mentally ill. All I could focus on was that, finally, no-one could have a go at me for being fat. I certainly had no conception of the decade-long nightmare that awaited me. I returned the next day and was given a blood test form to take to Leicester Royal Infirmary. After the test I walked the three miles back to the Halls of Residence, but found my pace slowing as I went along. Eventually I ground to a halt and blacked out on the side of the road.

For the next couple of weeks I began to settle into the life of being an anorexic, eating less and less and isolating myself more and more. While I waited to be referred to an eating disorder specialist, I went to see one of the University counsellors, whose sole piece of wisdom was that "cars can't run without fuel". Well I could run without fuel, I had proved that before and would prove it again. I don't remember ever being scared or worried or embarrassed by Anorexia's appearance in my life. To be honest it was more a case of pride, excitement and confidence. Now I really was "someone", now I finally had licence to eat and to sit around and now, at last, I was a success at something which people thought was worthwhile. I was thin and the whole world could see it. No more Mr Average.

My parents were due to visit, and they seemed particularly anxious to come to Leicester once I told them about my diagnosis. I was actually quite looking forward to seeing them. They would be staying at a hotel quite a way away and, while I would probably be expected to have a meal with them at some point, they wouldn't be able to tell me what to eat at any other time. Also, they were bringing my scales with them, so that I could keep an eye on my weight and check it wasn't going any lower. When I opened the door, the look on my mother's face told me that she wasn't going to share my fondness for Anorexia.

Once my parents had seen me, they couldn't get me home quick enough and it was agreed with my Doctor that I should take a two week break from University. Despite myself, I was beginning to make friends in my Halls and I again cannot deny the warm inner glow I felt in being able to tell them of my achievement. It's only now that I can appreciate how difficult it must have been for them. The first year at University is meant to be about partying and drinking and spending all night working on essays to hand in the morning after. It is not meant to be about someone who you've only just met turning round and saying "Hi, by the way I'm anorexic and I've got to go home for a bit of a rest. Cheers for being such great mates. Have some chocolates".

I went back to Wales with my parents, stopping off for chips on the way. This was going to be great—I was being given permission to eat! Now I had been given a name to put to my problem and I could prove that I hadn't been as unfit as I had feared, it felt like I had acquired an extra layer of confidence to replace the doubt. Being seen to be thin had become so important to me that Anorexia appeared like manna from heaven—a cast-iron defence against "Jonah the Whale" ever making a reappearance. I had bought myself a book on eating disorders and it was almost a thrill to be able to tick off the symptoms and behaviours as I read through it. The book made reference to recovery cycles measured in years, of inpatient treatment and even of the possibility of death, but clearly that did not apply to me. All I needed to do was to put on a little weight and I would be fine.

Had I appreciated quite how grave my illness was, I doubt I would have treated my diagnosis with quite so much equanimity, but in my ignorance I was confident that a couple of weeks off studying and a bit of my Mum's cooking would soon have me back on my feet. Something happened, though, in those two weeks that I spent mostly sat in front of the fire covered in blankets, whereby I became more and more conscious of my world seeming to shrink around me. I have never received more sweets and chocolates in my life and never felt so utterly incapable of eating even the smallest mouthful. As a succession of friends came to visit, I became increasingly withdrawn and felt like I was on display, particularly when I was being fed in their presence. My parents did all they could to make things easy for me and to give me food they knew I liked, but all I wanted to do was to escape back to Leicester. I could sense my parents' horror whenever they looked at me and my sister was similarly appalled when she saw me for the first time. I thought if they read the book I had bought it would all become as easily understandable to them as it was to me—what I was feeling, why I couldn't just 'snap out of it', why I had to exercise—but it just seemed to make them angry.

Soon the time came to head back to Leicester. Now my secret was out, I knew things would have to change, and I was happy to be going back to begin the first stages of my recovery. I was determined, however, that it should be 'my recovery', done in my own way and on my terms. While I waited for my referral to the Brandon Mental Health Unit at Leicester General Hospital, I resolved to follow doctor's orders, drinking plenty of fluid and eating little and often. As "Anorexic John", I knew I would have friends, as well as staff from the Halls and from University looking out for me, in addition to my regular appointments with my Doctor. However, as the weeks turned to months, the more I began to realise I would not 'snap out of it' and the more I read my book and connected with everything in it, the harder and harder it became to resist the voice in my head. Yes I was thin, but what if my weight went out of control once I began restoring? If I did no exercise, surely my fitness levels would be eroded irrevocably?

The difference now was that I was answering these questions as an anorexic, which left no room for any thought of challenging my assumptions that "Food=Fat, Exercise=Fit". I had agreed to limit my exercise to a couple of walks a day, but I retained the management of my food intake, and I knew that if I had a full plate or a 'fatty' meal, it would all be my fault, that I would have to cope with the guilt. By now my University work had really begun to suffer, I was continuing to isolate myself and my friend from school had disappeared into his own social world. I felt more and more alone and never in less control of anything other than what I ate and how I looked.

More than ever before, Anorexia offered me the security and confidence I was not getting anywhere else.

KIMMERIDGE COURT DIARY
WEEK 3

Now I was firmly settled back in to Kimmeridge Court, the first cracks were beginning to appear in the relentless positivity I felt regarding my recovery. Getting out for walks was a massive relief after days of virtual nothingness, but it didn't take me long to look upon my once-daily "exercise" as a must-do, ritualistic activity. Bad weather meant we were not always allowed out and I was getting back in the old routine of standing by the window, urging the rain to stop so I could be released. Very early on in my admission, it was clear that I would have to start addressing issues that were left alone four years ago.

Friday 1 January: Day 19

Chips—previous dislike, everything wrong and my choice. As soon as I ticked the box last night, I could feel Anorexia kicking in. Chips to me have always represented everything that is wrong—fat, filling, society's ultimate 'bad food'. To CHOOSE it—over mash and rice—to opt for this unhealthy rubbish suddenly raised the old worries—it's unhealthy, it'll make you put on weight, it's all fat—feelings that I've largely managed to suppress in my first three weeks. I rationalised my concerns by telling myself that gaining weight is the point of being here, that it will be another challenge, that eating to enjoy as opposed to eating for health is something that I have to bring to my diet. And, you know, chips (and brown sauce, another challenge!) was ok, even nice. I haven't expanded, the world hasn't collapsed and I'm going out later (hopefully). That's what I have to focus on and look forward to. I don't know what it is that's different—I'm not even sure that I didn't feel exactly the same during my last admission—but I genuinely feel more ready to change now. So far to go, but don't look back. PMA.

Good Stuff—Keir's visit was really good. A welcome glimpse of the real world.

Saturday 2 January: Day 20

If I'm honest with myself, I feel no fatter at 44.5kg than I did at 42kg. Whether that's just because I'm still talking low weights I'm not sure, but (touch wood) the guilty feeling has yet to rear its head. Perhaps I need to take a more positive view on my recovery i.e. not "what can I do to stay healthy" but more "what can I do now I am healthy". Contrary to what I have believed, the chips and the extra coleslaw I had yesterday are not preying on my mind. I should be fretting, agitated until next weigh day so that I can comfort myself that the world hasn't fallen in.

Life is there if I choose to grab it.

Sunday 3 January: Day 21

Not a great day today and I could have done without the support (*from staff*) at the meal table. When I have a meal of that size I just have to keep my focus, and I did well not to compare what was on my plate with anyone else's. As with yesterday I just have to fight any negative feelings I have at the moment—I am going to feel disgusting whatever—and keep on keeping on. Truth is the meal—mash potato on top of spaghetti bolognese is almost all carbs, so has to be bulky to get enough calories. I don't feel overfull after it and it is all going towards the greater good, isn't it? If I am as committed as I have claimed then things like this cannot be allowed to stress me out. Short-term pain = long-term gain.

Day ended better with pub quiz. That is what LIFE is about—going out, being with people I like and not worrying about my figure. I have to keep pushing the boundaries, taking risks or this is all for nothing.

Good stuff—Quiz, no full stomach and Leeds beat Man. Utd!

Monday 4 January: Day 22

BMI: 16.0

Not quite sure where my head is at. I anticipated the eating part of my recovery to be less painful than the exercise, but I'm actually finding myself looking forward to meals and able to cope with things like yesterday which a short time ago would have totally freaked me out. The manner in which I have accepted my weight gain is completely alien—is it just because it's not solely of my doing, is it because I have yet to break 45kg and all my fears will re-emerge at that point? Can it really be true that my thinking has changed to such an extent that the overriding fear that has dominated my life for fourteen years no longer seems to matter so much?

The exercise remains a greater concern and, while I can happily contemplate not walking for hours in the wind and the rain, can I begin to believe that I could go a whole day without exercise? Could I sit on a train for hours and not cut back on my eating? Can I wash-up, hang out my washing, do my job, use the computer, do the ironing, do the shopping etc, in any other way than the anorexic, ritualistic manner that I have done for years? Honestly, at the moment the answer would be no. In Kimmeridge I can sit down ok—the fatigue is still there acting like an anchor on my body—but any time there is a prospect of exercise—food management, snack out, going home—those urges return. I'm not sure if it's because I see a direct link to my weight, or because I feel the need to be seen to be active, or whether the urge within me to be constantly on the move is so overwhelming. Cracking this exercise thing is the key to my recovery and hopes for a healthy life. I do still believe, more than I have done for a long time, but it is going to be very, very hard to change my default settings.

I don't actually like my body. It's horrible, skeletal, painful, pathetically weak and limits me in almost every aspect of my life. Nor do I recoil at the idea of being a healthy weight, a BMI 20—though any higher would not be good. The problem I foresee is that, horrible and sad looking my body may be, it is the body I have had for half my life, the one I have struggled with, run with, bent over with, showered with and of which I know every bony, protruding edge. It is not the thought of how I will look at BMI 20 but how will I feel to walk around in a body that will not be 'healthy' to my mind but which will be fatter, fleshier, maybe even bouncier than I can remember? Can I go beyond the first grab, first inch pinched, first wobble of fat and maintain my focus to the end? Last time I maintained my focus until I reached my target, but found that when I got there I could neither handle the feeling nor resist the urge to go back to old routines and to begin testing the limits of what my new body could achieve. At the moment a life without walks, scales, calorie-counting and 'freedom' still seems a long way away and I have absolutely no idea of how I will get there. All I know is that I DO WANT TO GET THERE and the only thing I can think to do is to keep going, to not look back and maintain PMA. Just keep going.

I do still worry that I appear to be too comfortable with things at the moment, almost as if I feel as though I need to justify my place here, but if they (*other patients*) had lived inside my anorexic head then there would be no question. I need to hear things like that (*praise for accepting an offer of a chip from a staff member at the meal table*), lord knows I'm not exactly overburdened with compliments, and healthy people do not freak out when they receive them. I know this is only three weeks, I have so far to go it's unreal, but these people don't live or die by my progress, so their compliments, as opposed to those of friends and family surely are sincere.

All this over a chip!

Good stuff—Food Management, the chip, talking to Davina and Erin (*nurses*), watching a DVD, believing there's hope, Robyn's thanks. The whole damn day has been good for me.

Tuesday 5 January: Day 23

God, I'm thin—I need to keep seeing myself in the mirror first thing in the morning to remind me of that fact. Plus my backside hurts and that is not healthy.

I can sense the doubts of people here and I can't query them, not until I walk the walk. To prove myself I have to cope with days of less exercise + more food i.e. a "healthy person's" day. I can do it. I WILL DO IT.

I hope I can look back on today as significant. Erin was right—she always is—I have been using my walks as a new routine, an excuse to exercise and it is exactly that which I need to escape from. I hate having empty days, sitting around doing trivial stuff, so I have to focus and get out of here in a way that will allow me never to return. My Anorexia is telling me that today is wrong, that I will be eating too much and not doing anything to compensate for that, but I need to allow my life to include days like this, because that is what healthy people do—not gym monkeys or anorexics—but HEALTHY people, who don't care about running, or calories, or what other people think. They don't care.

I would be betraying so many people by not pulling through on this one. Sod that, though. I need to focus on ME and what this means to ME, and I can just about glimpse the possibility of a better life. It is there for me, but at the moment it's just words. I'm feeling a bit mixed up at the moment, and the thought of my sandwich tonight fills me with dread, but still I can't help feeling like smiling. This may all blow up in my face. I may not be able to handle it and I may wake up tonight desperate to escape, but it feels like an important day. The mere idea of not going out for a walk because I DON'T WANT TO and because I don't have to and because I know it's what I have to do at this moment, it seems both completely not "John" and actually quite satisfying. I don't want to live a sedentary lifestyle and I have it in my power to live life as I wish, but that is the point—LIVE LIFE. Looking forward is suddenly so exciting.

Today is ground zero, everything from now on is a new challenge, and while I know tough days will come, they're not going to be much tougher than this and I'm smiling at the moment. There's a whole world out there, beyond food and exercise and bed rest and Kimmeridge Court. PMA, don't look back, keep focused.

> Good stuff—Ate at posh cafe (£14 for two drinks + two cakes!), spoke to Hannah. DIDN'T GO FOR A WALK!

Wednesday 6 January: Day 24

Fortunately the weather in the early stages of my self-imposed imprisonment is awful—it's easier to be stuck indoors when the snow and ice mean there's a risk of physical injury if you step outside. Again I feel thin, if not quite as thin, and happy in the choice I have made. What I said (*in Health Awareness group*) this morning is true. The physical effects of this can, and will, be rectified, but it is the emotional and mental beliefs underpinning the illness that have to be tackled if long-term recovery is a remote possibility. A lot of what I am being told is preaching to the converted. I know all this, the downsides of the illness, what it gives me, what it takes away, the fact that some die, that many, many more never recover their full potential, but it is never enough to beat the power it holds, the comfort and the pleasure it gives me.

As Anorexics, we all hold the power to 'snap out of this', to take control of our lives and yet we feel and believe ourselves to be among the least powerful and least in control people in the world. Certainly until very recently I had abandoned hope and if there is one thing this illness does it is to suck the hope out of you. Maybe I'm wrong and I did feel like this four years ago, but I don't remember seeing a glimpse of light. Other people will remain dubious, and with good reason, but before trying to convince them I need to convince myself. I have to be comfortable in my own skin. Recovery, if it ever happens, will still be a long term battle. I'll have shit days and shittier days, and more than once I will seek a return to the safety that Anorexia gives me. What if I am still rubbish at work? What if my weight does start to rise? What happens the first time someone says I'm "looking better"? What happens when I have a day with nothing to do, no plans, no structure beyond the food that will have to be compensated for? So much still to prove.

Thursday 7 January: Day 25

BMI: 16.1

Bad things about calorie counting

1) I get really anxious when calorie rules are broken
2) It doesn't allow any room for treats or spontaneity
3) It makes me anxious when eating with other people—"Are they eating less than me?"
4) It limits my social life and the number of places I can eat in
5) Means I can't eat food cooked by other people
6) Has major detrimental physical impact
7) Creates boundaries in life which are there to be tested
8) Reinforces my pre-occupation with food

Benefits of not calorie-counting

1) Freedom—to eat different foods in different places, without the need to exercise
2) Better social life
3) Ability to be spontaneous
4) Lower anxiety levels
5) Less of a focus on food

How to feel about today? I suppose it's inevitable that days like this will occur—this was never going to be a smooth path to happiness. The more positive I feel, the more I can sense the Anorexia beckoning me to return to old ways, reminding me of what it feels like to believe in your own worthlessness. I almost cringe inside when I hear myself in groups sometimes, spouting positivity when I still hold so many doubts about myself. I just have to keep questioning every thought as it occurs—What will standing up achieve? What am I missing out on when Anorexia is my life? When I know you need so many extra calories every day to put on weight, what difference will one snack make? Typically, I want everything now, this instant, but there is so far to go it's unreal. Why would butter in my mash potato freak me out? Can I really live a life without calories, given how much I already know? Can I find enough in my life to fill the gaps between meals? I so want this time to be different, and I truly believe it can be.

PMA, son, PMA.

THE WORK/LIFE IMBALANCE

The rest of my time at University passed by in a blur: a hugely wasted opportunity. For years I would boast about leaving University with no debt, convinced that it provided yet more evidence of extreme powers of self-control. I don't think there's anything I would like more now than to say I was still up to my ears in student debt, because at least it would have meant I hadn't spent three years feeding my Anorexia. And while I kept working, kept battling the illness in my own way, I never did anything to address any of the underlying issues behind my Anorexia, nor to establish a life for myself outside of its presence. I kept the same room—Room 29, Block 8—throughout my three years in halls and after my nightly walk, spent most evenings on my own, my friends from the first year having moved out into the City Centre. I was seeing my Eating Disorders Counsellor on a regular basis, dutifully filling out my food diary and recording my daily thoughts which usually amounted to how hard I was finding it to change but also how determined I was to do just that. My mood fluctuated depending on what I'd eaten and whether I had done "enough" exercise—fine and dandy if I knew I'd lived my day to plan and within my limits, but any slight feeling of having lost control would send my emotions spiralling.

As at many times throughout my relationship with Anorexia, exercise was at this time not something I enjoyed but acted merely as a means to an end, both allowing me to eat and provided brief respite from the otherwise constant worries about food and my shape. Rain, wind, snow, ice, none of it made walking very pleasurable but the sense of comfort that surrounded me once I was back inside kept me going, as did the fear of how I would feel if I wimped out. As my weight increased, my activity levels followed suit, eventually including cycling to university, rejoining the gym and finally having that game of football, and I managed to maintain a pattern of eating sufficient to keep my weight stable. I was discharged after three years, firmly of the belief that I had been 'cured' but without any real understanding of what that meant.

For the final year I threw myself into my work, and this distracted me from my thoughts and allowed me to structure my days around study rather than mealtimes. My parents seemed assured of my recovery and began to trust me a bit more, although a degree of tension remained. As has been a constant throughout my illness, I was forever urging them to trust me and to believe me when I said I was ok, that I really was trying and that I was happy at last. However, I never found within myself the ability to trust them, and still occasionally Anorexia convinces me that I am being watched, that my mother wants to fatten me up, that they are completely ashamed of me and angry at what I have put them both through.

When I returned home during the holidays I would always want to make absolutely sure what we were having for tea so that I could prepare myself and to plan my day and my other meals around how many calories I would later consume. I hung around the kitchen to check that no hidden extras were being added to the promised menu and it became especially important to me that Dad would have a larger portion than I did. Still surrounded by the dark fog of my Anorexia, one extra chip on my plate would be the difference between feeling safe and calm and happy or being scared and angry and being completely unable to think of anything else but food and my weight, at least until I had sought out the reassurance of the scales.

Absolved in my mind of any excuses not to succeed, I was bitterly disappointed that I only achieved a 2:1 in my History degree. I didn't view my Anorexia as being sufficiently strong to have affected my studies to any real extent, and the result proved to me that I had not worked hard enough. I was fit again though and began to throw myself back into my sport when I returned home, joining the local football team and again walking my Uncle's dog—which, after all, was legitimate exercise. In recognition of my "recovery", I had been bought a rowing machine and this again quickly became a daily ritual, always when I was alone at home so no-one could comment on whether I was doing too much. I was back to days of not sitting down if at all possible and seeking to use my rediscovered fitness as a base from which to become even fitter. The rules upon which Anorexia had built my downward spiral remained intact: no treats, no eating between meals and absolutely no wasted opportunities to burn those calories.

I had now entered the job market, with little idea of where to go other than that the thought of sitting another exam seemed too exhausting even to contemplate. I had started a part-time job in the local greengrocers during my holidays from university, and I continued this on a more-or-less full-time basis while looking for a career. I enjoyed my job there working for two of the nicest, most genuine people I have ever met, and it gave me the opportunity to be with people all day. Only when I was left in charge on Wednesday afternoons was my Anorexia really allowed to manifest itself, as I spent the generally quiet four hours restacking carrots from the warehouse one by one and walking up and down the shop floor reading my newspaper. In the meantime, I also finally passed my driving test, at the fourth attempt. This gave me a greater high than any of my academic achievements, which had almost felt automatic. I hated driving, and had considered giving up many times, so to succeed at something in which my brain was of little or no use was a huge boost. Clearly, though, as driving involved sitting down for long periods of time, this was a new skill to be employed only on very rare occasions.

As my search for a new job stretched into the New Year I could sense my parents' impatience hardening, and I became more conscious of the need to find something fairly soon. History degrees are ideal for very few occupations but do offer transferable skills that can be useful in many areas, and I decided to seek out my 'dream job' in football. My search encompassed dozens of feeler letters to clubs and broadcasters, with those who did reply unable to give me much hope. My journalistic career to this point amounted to three articles published in the Leicester University Student Newspaper, the demands of my illness having prevented me from doing the kind of voluntary spadework that can often provide that vital 'foot in the door'. Concluding that my parents' patience was receding quickly, I took a job with CIS Insurance in Manchester, determined to take advantage of moving to the big city. What I really moved back to was life as a fully fledged anorexic.

Although my weight had stayed fairly steady in the year after graduation, the core beliefs that underpinned my Anorexia remained intact. The pride I had in my illness continued to shine through, especially when my mum talked about other people she knew who had been affected. Her aim was, I'm sure, to offer me strength, but all I felt was jealousy. No-one else was allowed to be the anorexic in our lives, that was my role and it was one I did not yet feel ready to let go. Whilst everyone assumed I was cured, I was still beset with the same thoughts and preoccupations that were just waiting for the opportunity to rear their head again. My new job was based four miles from home, a perfect distance to cycle in every day. My office was on the sixth floor, close enough to the ground for me to feel justified in using the stairs as opposed to the lift. Best of all, the building housed a gymnasium that was free to all employees, so every Friday and Sunday, without fail, I would be there following the carefully devised fitness programme set out for me whilst I was at University. I was often in there alone, although on occasion I would be sharing with the gym monkeys as they flexed their muscles in front of the floor-to-ceiling mirrors. I had no connection with them, either in their desire to build muscle upon muscle or in feeling I had anything really to admire other than my sure fire knowledge that I looked better than I had three years before. The company also supplied free meals so I was still eating ok, at least initially, but my exercise soon began getting out of control. After a short time the experience of eating with my colleagues in our dinner hour became more and more stressful, especially when any of them left anything on their plates. I dressed up my distress in terms of the food they were wasting, but inside Anorexia was screaming at me for over-eating.

I lived for the days at work when I would be on "journeys", delivering internal post every couple of hours to the various departments across all 24 floors. This allowed for numerous trips up and downstairs, which of course didn't count as exercise because it was for work, and lots of time away from my chair, where every second sat down was another calorie added. With so many colleagues in the office, birthdays were a regular event and sweets and chocolate bars were always offered round. The thought of actually eating them in front of the others, in between meals, never crossed my mind. How weak and greedy would that make me look? I had to be the one who demonstrated willpower, as that would mark me out from the rest as someone of strength and self-pride. I was certainly not distinguishing myself through my work, menial though most of it was, as I had quickly established a pattern of exercising in any way possible, taking files from my desk to the cupboard one by one and standing up when using the phone. As all jobs within the office were time-measured, I was usually bottom of the pile, but I saw no choice but to stick to my regime and managed to bluff my way through every appraisal with promises to do better.

If the weekends were not taken up by cycling to work to do overtime, I would literally spend every waking hour on my feet, walking back and forth to Manchester and different points in between. Every night after work I would run to the local superstore and back before an hour's walk after tea to "let the food settle". This would usually take me down Manchester's "Curry Mile", a seemingly endless procession of Asian restaurants, shops and music stores which provided a cavalcade of colour and noise every evening. I gazed into the windows of the sweet shops (never stopping still, though, for I had to keep walking) all the while knowing I could never allow myself to give in to temptation. I would check the plates of people in the restaurants, getting a buzz off the fact that they were in there, stuffing their faces whilst I was outside, walking, being fit and slim.

After a year, I began to tire of insurance customers phoning me in work specifically to instruct me to shove their payment cheques up my arse. Living in Manchester was great, although I did not make anywhere near as much of it as I should have done and I didn't really make any friends while I was there. My work colleagues had begun to comment on my weight and, when my boss asked me if anything was wrong, I gave him chapter and verse about my Anorexia. Now the cat was out of the bag, my ability to continue as I had been at work would obviously be severely curtailed, so the time had come to move on. I again began to search for my dream job and came across a post for a Football Development Administrator with the local County Football Association. Another impeccable interview—with no mention of my Anorexia—and the job was mine. The feeling when I read my job offer was the closest I've had to a high in the last fourteen years. I celebrated by going for a long walk.

Thanks for the Manchester Memories. Good luck for the future. Please dine well.

Don

KIMMERIDGE COURT DIARY
WEEK 4

January brought with it a proper case of Man Flu, which as always exacerbated the anorexic thoughts that were starting to return in tandem with a healthier weight. I was beginning again to question the motives behind my every action and every declaration in groups or in private conversation. Were my messages of support for their benefit or for mine? I was, though, continuing to make positive, unheard off decisions (paying for a taxi!), and reaching BMI 16 did at least mean I could join the others on social outings. Yet more freedom!

Friday 8 January: Day 26

I'm three and a half weeks in and the first doubts are really beginning to surface. My cold doesn't help, but I'm beginning to appreciate how tough this is going to be. I act as if nothing bothers me, but at the moment that's the only way I can think of coping. If I begin to question what I'm doing, what is in front of me, I am worried that the guilt will return. I have run out of answers and if this doesn't work then I don't know what I am going to do.

Very mixed Managing Emotions group. Volunteering my decision not to go for a walk unless I need to as an example for CBT brought about a lot of negative emotions, especially guilt (am I over-egging it?; why do I want others to know?; why should I dominate group?; am I trying to belittle everyone else?) and increased anxiety over the lack of exercise. Are they laughing at me for being so "positive", do they see in me what I see in others? There is definitely part of me that worries that people will see me as a faker because I act so positive, but then I don't like to reveal my insecurities about my recovery because I don't feel like these concerns are commensurate with other peoples'.

But if I keep believing, keep challenging my thoughts keep looking forward and stay focused on why I am here, what I have to do and the benefits that will arise from it, then I will beat this, off my own back, because it is what I want. Let's be honest, everything I've experienced over the last four weeks is this

1) I can control my exercise levels without feeling guilty.
2) My weight has not ballooned despite eating large amounts, limiting exercise and taking risks.
3) Taking risks and taking control has left me with a sense of empowerment.
4) I can have a good time with my parents when food and exercise is not the issue.
5) Occasional treats are not bad for me—in fact for me they are quite the opposite.
6) If I make positive rather that negative choices this makes me feel good about myself.
7) One key to recovery is to take the next step beyond doing what is necessary, to make changes and to BELIEVE that recovery is possible.
8) I have proper, genuine friends.
9) The people at Kimmeridge, staff and patients, don't need me to get better, so all expressions of friendship and support must be genuine.
10) Negative feelings, physical and emotional, can be turned around and they pass and I have a blank canvas in the future.

The difference being in here is that in here I am not John the Anorexic, John the Freak, John the Weakling, John the Outsider. Here I'm just John; the difference between me and the others is not what I look like, how thin I am, how much exercise I do, but rather the personal traits and qualities that I have as John.

Saturday 9 January: Day 27

Days like today are the reason I have to keep fighting—unless I give up my Anorexia, I cannot meet Hannah for coffee, walking leisurely around the shops and not worrying about how far or how fast we go. I've had a great afternoon, precisely because I felt able to spend time with my best mate, and that is what life is about. What would be better: a happy, fit guy or a sad, lonely, thin guy? There is no competition.

Good snack out. Tried a milkshake for the first time ever (toffee caramel fudge) then, having missed my bus I paid £7 for a taxi rather than walking around for 45 minutes in the cold. Those are the type of decisions I have to make, the type that sensible, healthy people make every day of their sensible, healthy lives. I certainly feel more relaxed and if there's only one thing that has come out of this then it's that my friendship with Hannah has been reinforced. She has been more of a friend to me than I can say and the only blessing this illness has given me is that it has brought her into my life. Thing is, I feel as if recovery would actually be good for ME. I want to do it not just for Hannah, my family, my health, my job and my mates, but actually for ME. Days like today are what it's all about, it's why I came back (*to Kimmeridge*) and it's why this time I will get there. It will be the hardest thing I have EVER done to beat this but, hell, if it was easy I would have done it before now. I might never run a marathon, play up front for Everton or win any body-building contests, but if I can just learn to love myself, to recognise the qualities I have instead of looking to portray myself as some kind of health freak, I will be more healthy and less freaky. I can do this and I will do this.

PMA. Look forward not back. Keep your FOCUS.

Good stuff—meeting Hannah, having a milkshake, getting a taxi, finding that book I've been after for AGES, a point at Arsenal!

Sunday 10 January: Day 28

Emotions all over the shop again. If I'm honest, what Mum said about me (*at Christmas*) was absolutely true—I have always run away, always tried to outpace the Anorexia instead of meeting it head on. If I never challenge the Anorexia, how can I hope to beat it? Just waiting and hoping it will go away has never worked. Pushing the illness only as far as *the illness* would allow only provided temporary relief. I just feel like I need to keep pushing, maintain the momentum that I have built up. At the same time I'm wary of going too quickly and creating false hopes and expectations, especially when I see my parents. Can I really let them down again? I'd love them to share the excitement and optimism that I have at the moment, but can I really expect them to be anything other than sceptical? Even the staff here clearly have their doubts—maybe they think I'm hiding something—but it's not a "sod them" proving point with them, I simply want to repay them for all the help they have given to me by proving that this can work.

I can never hope to repay my parents for everything they've done for me, all I can do is try to make them happy.

At the end of the day (literally) I feel positive. Another day without exercise, and we'll just have to see what the scales say tomorrow. They definitely still hold some fears for me, and my default setting is still against weight gain, but again today there were enough positives to make it all seem worth it. This remains a very scary thing that I am undertaking, but is also exciting and filled with such potential that it would be criminal to give up without giving everything I have.

Good stuff—snack out, meeting Keir, making people smile

Monday 11 January: Day 29

BMI: 16.2

Again, mixed feeling over my weight this morning. At BMI 16 I really am entering unchartered territory and this is starting to raise all manner of old thoughts and demons. This is when the hard work really begins and it already feels as if the momentum is beginning to slide. There will be more food and yet more opportunity to exercise as I get nearer to "normality", so now it is even more important that I maintain my focus. I've had glimpses of a better life these past few days and, whilst activity is going to play a role in my life, *there is no need for it to become my life*. A 0.4kg increase since Thursday is nothing, especially considering two snack outs and minimal exercise. I have to remember this week in the future when I'm having a tough time and I'm worried about my weight—and those times will happen. My body is not unique, it is not a constantly expanding mass but it does need fuel to stay alive and even more to look vaguely healthy and to feed my mind enough to be *John*.

Another day without ½ hour walk and then sitting down and watching a whole film, but how long I can keep this going I don't know. I haven't proved myself capable at all of carrying through with my promises or my enthusiasm and I understand others' scepticism, but I DON'T SHARE IT. There is something different this time, something new and something stronger which is telling me that this can be beaten. I can't leave it behind completely, because it has been such a huge part of my life, but I can leave it in the past. This journey was only meant to last six weeks but has already taken fourteen years and it is now time to get off.

Being here (*at Kimmeridge*) continually rams home the harm this illness can do. There is absolutely no discrimination—young, old, mothers, students, athletes, artists—it is strong and persistent and crushing and it absolutely will not let go. Anorexia will hold on to you for dear life and the only way to get away is to let go yourself. Yes I will be thrown into the whirlwind of the unknown, but whilst this will be scary it may also be brilliant. In order to have a chance to experience life, I have to let go of Anorexia's hand. I will have more days like this, where I do little exercise, where I make positive choices which nonetheless cause anxiety and give rise to all the old worries, but I have to maintain my focus. I have only been here four weeks. Every time I challenge myself, every bit extra I have and every time I don't exercise it helps me move on. I have no other answers and no other solutions, but I trust the staff here and I DO BELIEVE.

Tuesday 12 January: Day 30

Just returned from social outing number one—how do I feel? Great to get out, but how much of it is the exercise? I think I got as much of a buzz off shopping as I did the walking but there is something still there. I don't think that will go until I prove myself in the 'real world', until then every day is an experiment at the moment. The fact is that right now I remain afraid of being fat, of the ridicule and insinuation that I believe would follow and I am unsure of my ability to resist Anorexia in the long term. I don't feel sufficiently strong to cope with setbacks in any other way than retreating to the safety of my Anorexia, and this is why I can't get ahead of myself. As I said before, I have no answers. I just feel as if there is a way out, and to get there I need to trust people and let them lead me until I can take on the challenge myself.

Wednesday 13 January: Day 31

Thinking again about all the situations in which I feel tension and anxiety surrounding food, it is those involving my parents that feature most prominently. I suppose this is because I associate them with being watched, having extra added to my meals, commenting when I leave food, having to wait for me to finish. It's strange though that I feel more comfortable in front of my sister, even though she has perhaps been the one least willing to indulge my Anorexia. With other people, the fears are more that they will think I'm a pig and at the very least I would make a point of eating less and going for the lowest calorie option. I think part of the problem with my parents—and they are clearly the people who care the most—is that I don't want them to think everything is ok, and it is certainly true that my behaviours become more exaggerated when I'm around them. On a good day I can put this down as not wanting to raise their expectations, but if I'm honest I still use the Anorexia as a mark of distinction, something which guarantees the attention which I crave.

I really don't want to blow this, so I have to maintain the challenges, because each one is a chip off the illness' grip. Anorexia hates being challenged, hates it every time I sit down, eat, enjoy myself instead of indulging it, and that is why I've got to view every such action as a double hit and every lapse as a double setback. I realise more than ever what I can have if I take the opportunity, and the damage that Anorexia has done to me has again been reiterated (*in Health Awareness talk on osteoporosis*). As of this moment I can see the light at the end of the tunnel and I'm aiming that way. Will I be doing the same in a month's time? Let's see.

PMA. Look forward not back. Keep focused.

Thursday 14 January: Day 32

BMI: 16.6

Well, that was unexpected! One kg put on in three days, a record even for me! It is a bit of a shock going from worrying about adding a snack to thinking about one being taken away, and my Anorexia is definitely kicking in now, telling me I'm fat, that I need to exercise, that I've lost control. I just have to keep trusting the staff and I definitely have to get out of the habit of weighing myself so often when I get home. The only way I can escape the obsession of day-to-day checking is not to check at all, to allow my body to manage itself. Everyone else ticks along, often eating worse and exercising less than I will do, and while I might not go done in history as an Adonis, I have a chance to be something more than poor, weak, anorexic John. To do that, I have to ride with the punches now, accept my medicine and try to normalise my behaviours and actions. Yes this weight gain does appear to confirm my beliefs, but I am dealing in extremes. I need to experience a healthy life in order to live a healthy life. Keep looking forward.

The hard work will start soon, as my body develops a healthier look and I can feel myself getting closer to a healthier state. The point of limiting my exercise is so that I can reinforce the idea that exercise is a part of life, not the point of life. If I want to live, then I cannot allow exercise to become such a dominant factor in my existence. My obsession left no room for anything else, no light amidst the darkness. Talking in these terms is slightly superficial, but if it helps to emphasise the bleakness of that existence then it will do.

Why do I care so much about what people think? I'm not even sure it's people who know me, but people in general, what their first impression will be. Logic tells me that the anorexic look is not a winner, but because of society's view, because of my own prejudices, my fear about being fat is grounded massively in what people say. I know that by continuing to live my life according to how others view me I am letting the bullies win. I have always known this and I'm aware that I need to turn my anger towards shoving it back in their face. I've let them win for long enough, it is time to leave them in the past, with all the sadness and the lies and the missed opportunities. It's time to grab life.

I've always said that my first admission was the hardest thing that I have ever done, but it was easy against what I'm doing now. I've risked humiliation, my job, "coming out" to my friends, my self-respect and my relationship with my parents and as yet I don't know if it'll be worth it, but while I possess a grain of determination, I will fight like I've never fought before.

PMA. Forward not back. Focus.

WHY ME?

It's something that I have thought a lot about, but pinning down the reasons why Anorexia chose me is something I don't think I will ever definitively accomplish. I can point to bullying, low self-esteem, perfectionism, O.C.D. tendencies and an obsession with sport, but these are factors in the lives of hundreds of thousands of people, most of whom go on to live healthy lives. I was always the sensible one, so it was even more shocking to find myself completely crushed by a mental illness, to the extent that all my focus, all my willpower was directed to the pursuit of one goal—preventing weight gain—to the detriment of family, work, social lives and, of course, physical and mental well-being. Once my Anorexia took hold, it created circumstances—increased isolation, over-exercise, fasting, generating mistrust with family and friends—that allowed it to perpetuate itself to the extent that the illness became all-pervading, my greatest enemy and my greatest friend and always, always there. I knew that the solution to my "problem" was more food and less exercise, but these things were so alien, so abhorrent that the mere suggestion led to panic, suspicion and hostility towards those trying to help.

Exercise has always been the dominant partner in my relationship with Anorexia and I have maintained levels of activity beyond that which my body should really have been capable right up to the date of both inpatient admissions. I drove my body literally beyond the limit, and I could not find it within myself to rest even as my body was screaming out to me to stop. Only when I entered Kimmeridge Court and allowed the staff there to interrupt the dialogue within my head did my body get that chance to rest and only then did I realise how tired it was possible for someone to feel. It wasn't long after my first discharge that I forgot all about that overwhelming sense of tiredness and welcomed Anorexia back into my life, and even now it remains a continuing battle to keep the downsides of the illness at the forefront of my mind.

At times I found the strength from somewhere to reduce my exercise levels and I certainly found this easier to cope with than adding to my diet, but I never truly overcame Anorexia's all-encompassing nature, whereby every activity, every process was carried out in accordance with the ultimate commandment: 'thou shall not gain weight'. From the minute I woke to the moment I fell asleep, every thought and action was governed by my adherence to this rule: washing up, hanging clothes on the line, using the computer, posting letters, doing the shopping, opening the mail, cooking meals, cycling to work, doing my job, using the telephone, putting stuff out for recycling, going to the toilet, getting dressed; all these done in such a way as to burn as many calories as possible and to reduce the feelings of guilt at having eaten. And once you have done something in a particular way, walked round a certain corner or done an extra sit-up, you absolutely have to do exactly the same the next day and the next and the next. Failure to do so allows only one option: eat less.

Anorexia doesn't leave you, it doesn't go on breaks and there are no compromise solutions. I have seen it ruin lives, devastate families and drive some of the most gentle, caring people I have ever met to levels of self-abuse and self-hatred that crush the soul and it cannot be beaten back with a sticking plaster and a kiss better. It has taken fifteen years for me to even begin to accept recovery as a possibility for me and I can still offer no guarantees. I have greater belief than ever before in my ability to fight back and to live a life away from Anorexia's grim control, but I suspect that it will always be a factor in my life, even when hopefully it is no longer my reason for living.

KIMMERIDGE COURT DIARY
WEEK 5

A proper up and down week, with the highs of meeting friends and being given greater independence contrasting sharply with the realisation that issues of weight and exercise, especially in the shape of "massive" weight gain, was still sufficient to send my brain off in a haze of fear and confusion. My aim on admission had been to reach a maintenance target of BMI 20, but already I was beginning to question my ability to cope when I reached that point. I also doubted quite how popular I was on the unit, both with staff and patients, at the same time as other, more "manly" feelings were beginning to reappear.

Friday 15 January: Day 33

It's almost a running joke here that "John's fine". I don't talk in support, I don't seek conversations about my problems and I like to be seen as a strong base of support for others. Why? In support, it's just that I don't feel as if anyone is going to tell me something about myself that I haven't already thought of and recited to myself a thousand times. Others have their own problems, at this stage they would appear to be far greater than mine, and I would feel selfish if I felt I was taking up their time. Truth is I'm fed up with my own whining—I'm bored with talking about my parents and why they don't believe me—and I'm conscious of talking for talking's sake. I like the role I have here—solid, dependable, funny, "sorted",—and I hope this projects a positive image amongst the other patients. I can't apologise for enjoying the food and finding this stage of my recovery "easy" and I'm just happy that I don't have the struggle that others seem to. The hope that keeps me going is that everyone is right and that when I hit maintenance my weight will stabilise. I've always viewed maintenance as the difficult period but, although that will certainly be the time when I am most challenged, it could equally be enjoyable, a time to really focus on the future. At the same time, it is important that I don't treat maintenance as a two week wonder. I can't draw definitive conclusions until I've maintained for two, three months and beyond, after I've returned to work and a regular eating pattern. I believe it can happen, and I think I believe in myself, but first I have to get to BMI 20, ignore the physical changes and the image I "see" in the mirror.

You do get plunged deeper into the eating disorder here, though, and tiny little incidents can assume gargantuan proportions. The sense of achievement I've gained from adding tomato sauce to my meals has been ridiculous. Each tiny change to my physical state seems so massive, but this is where I need to take a breath and think logically. My body is not special!

I don't want to be here in 50 years' time, looking back with regret on my life as I have done on the last fourteen years. I am noticing physical changes and there are major fears over what I will be like at BMI 20, but think how much fitter, better looking, more concentrated I will be at that point too. Everything I've talked about—going to Australia, writing a book, moving back to Wales—it's all a load of hooey unless I keep on keeping on. I don't want my life back—I don't want anything of my old life—I need new goals, new things, a new me. It's there. Do I have the guts to risk everything and take a chance?

Good stuff—Hannah's good marks, eating in the INR (*independent kitchen*), kind words.

Saturday 16 January: Day 34

I have doubted my ability to exert any control over my life for so long that Anorexia has come to represent the only sure thing I can rely on. I may not be proud of my job, my qualifications, my personality but at least no-one can say that I'm fat. Written down like that it seems completely screwed, but when that is the only message you are hearing every day, it is difficult to dismiss. Even in the times when I have weight-restored, I haven't committed to the necessary changes to keep Anorexia out of my life, I haven't taken the risk of seeing what lies beyond the illness. I still ate in private, continued to exercise, wouldn't eat anything without knowing its calorie content—all this while saying I was "ok". Anorexia will grow stronger if it is not fought against, and I have both given up fighting and built so many barriers that no-one else can get close enough to help me.

I'm happy with today's snack out. There were definitely worrying echoes of the need to meet certain (*exercise*) targets, although I suppose each walk did have a purpose, and I did sit down where possible. At least I had plenty of time to relax and talk to Hannah, another reminder of how great a friend she is. If I mess up that friendship again then I'm a bigger fool than everybody thinks. Of most significance, I did not take the opportunity to get off a stop early—a tiny, miniscule thing, but nonetheless worth noting. I've really got to work hard to avoid complacency, but each little triumph is another step forward. Whatever I've done before, whatever steps I've previously taken, I now have a clean slate. Also tried a Mocha and a Cappuccino. New experiences every day!

Sunday 17 January: Day 35

Enthusiasm of last night has gone. I'm tired, worried about Australia and Mum's reaction and thus my concern has turned towards my 'six-pack' and today's food, which I anticipate being very heavy. No matter how much I drum home the message about being focused and putting on weight, there remains a nagging doubt about all this food. My financial situation doesn't help either, but if I'm going to spend money on anything then surely making snack out a regular thing is the way to go. There was a definite jolt when I saw my stomach this morning. I can't deny that having more flesh makes me look better, and 70 per cent of me is happy about that, but the remainder is screaming out to me that I'm getting fatter and that everything will career out of control.

The doubts are starting to return and this is the time to front up. It is said that if you confront bullies they will leave you alone. I have never confronted mine, and maybe that is why they never left me alone. If the worst case scenario occurs, at least I'll have the small satisfaction of having been proved right about my fat blimp of a body. But maybe, just maybe, I'll prove myself wrong, the bullies' power over me will be gradually chipped away, and I can finally move on. DO IT. Doubts remain, I am definitely beginning to notice physical changes and I would have been upset not to get out today. On the other hand; I didn't go the long way round; I chose what I wanted for snack, not the cheapest or lowest calorie option; most crucially I chose some extra ice cream tonight, not to put on weight, not as a challenge but because *I wanted it!* Really, really strange feeling, and worrying to a degree, but maybe a sign that my willpower is being slightly redirected. Also, seeing a former fellow patient, who I never anticipated would 'make it', look well and happy actually gave me quite a boost. If she can make it, so can I.

Once again, my libido is returning as my weight gradually restores. It's a strange by-product of Anorexia in that my sense of desire towards women almost completely disappears when I am at my lowest, but I suppose my hormone levels must get hit for six. Also, the isolation required for Anorexia to flourish is not conducive to any kind of meaningful relationship, of which my experience is embarrassingly limited. The problem with my 'sexual reawakening' occurring now whilst in the company of five or six attractive young women is that friendships forged over the opening weeks of my stay here can quickly be built up in my head into potentially something far bigger than is realistic or, in all honesty, desirable. As with my previous admission, I would be unbelievably lucky if any of these women knew that I existed, and the potential for two Anorexia's clashing, especially in such an early stage of recovery, is something that renders any kind of serious relationship, essentially unworkable. Plus it's against the rules! It is embarrassing, while every other part of me is looking forward to the future, I retreat to the role of shy schoolboy, hanging around the girl's corridor in an attempt to pay her a compliment. Still, you never know once my six-pack develops! PMA!

Monday 18 January: Day 36

BMI 17.1

I was not expecting that weight this morning and it has thrown my head into a bit of a whirl. These past five weeks have all been about limiting my exercise and challenging my beliefs about food—and now it feels as though everything has changed overnight. I felt so good yesterday that I was making what I considered to be positive choices (*about having* bad *foods*), indeed I was enjoying being able to make those choices, but virtually being told that I've been overeating has screwed me up. Has my willpower been shot to pieces? Should I now exercise every day? The voice in my head has certainly got louder and whilst it is a small comfort to get some justification for how fat I've been feeling these past few days, it seems as if my long-term fears are merely being confirmed. I don't want to lose a snack, that is my honest feeling and that should confirm that my Anorexia is being confronted, but do I feel ready to take that step (*start eating less*) and how much exercise will I need to do and how much can I do without it becoming ritualistic again? What if maintenance does not arrest the escalation in weight? I should be looking to add food as I go along, not have it taken away, but everything just seems to be accelerating. To be honest, I'd feel better if it was like it used to be, when even the suggestion of putting on weight would completely freak me out. At least I knew where I stood, whereas now I'm torn between being focused on recovery but also absolutely spinning and messed up and frightened, so, so frightened about what is happening with my weight.

What do I do now? Keep going for snack out, even though I don't *have* to have a snack? Go for a walk every day, even when I don't need to? All the positive changes I have made, all the boosts to my self-esteem and the good feelings that have been generated as a consequence, it has all been messed up in one step onto the scales. I hate the fact that after so much positive feeling, doubts have been allowed to creep in. I'm feeling hungry now and my brain is telling me it's because I've eaten too much, that I've lost control. Part of me does want to resist the urge to exercise, but even more so I just want to get out. Where everything was so sure I really don't know which way to turn. I'm also feeling crap for being so obviously 'unhappy'. What have I got to complain about compared with everyone else? Part of me wants to slap me for being so miserable, part of me is so, so confused with how I'm feeling at the moment Not great.

Having had a couple of hours' distraction and time to calm down, I've come to the following conclusions—whatever Thursday (*next weigh day*) brings will happen anyway, as of this moment I AM NOT FAT and that is the bottom line. I am now BMI 17 (hard though it is to believe, I'm still underweight) but to be honest I know I'm still not mentally with it. If I don't trust what I'm being told then I might as well abandon everything, and I'm not ready to give up hope yet. Everyone, healthy or not, has bad days and I've done well to get through five weeks before experiencing one. Speaking to Hannah really made me see things more clearly (again) and while my Anorexia will continue to scream blue murder at me, I have to gather the strength to keep fighting on. If that means calling on the support of others then do it, there is no shame in asking for help and I don't have to act the hard man all the time. Looking forward will inevitably breed uncertainty but it's about time I got some uncertainty in my life. Just swim with it.

That was a difficult meal tonight and I struggled with the pudding. Still, when told that I'd had more than I needed to, I did not take the opportunity to put some back. Why? Because if I start cutting back now, or going for a walk solely because I can, then everything I've achieved over the past five weeks has been for nothing. To turn back at the first hurdle would be "Anorexic John" to a tee, but unless I stop running away I will always be a little kid. Mummy is not going to protect me forever. Deal in facts—still underweight, barely BMI 17, very unwell. I am a patient in hospital with a mental illness. I am not Superman.

What has today taught me? That this is not going to be easy; that it is possible to eat too much (I knew it!); that I have to talk; that people care; that I can do this. After everything I've been thinking today I STILL DIDN'T GO FOR A WALK. I just think that's a tremendous achievement. If I can go a whole day without exercise, even when my entire being is screaming to get out, then I have it in me to beat this. PMA. Focus. Forward not back. I am worth it.

> Good stuff—getting through the day! Kind words and support, making people laugh, playing Scrabble. I can do this.

Tuesday 19 January: Day 37

Interesting question to come out of Recovery Group: Recovery versus Recovering? Recovering is, I think, a process towards the eventual goal of recovery. I have to be realistic in what I want to achieve here. I do believe, but to think that I can get to the point where the past fourteen years are an afterthought is hoping beyond hope. It will always be a factor in every decision I make, every relationship I forge and every time I reflect on my life. The key is to look upon it as a positive. It has been the hardest, most debilitating experience I will (hopefully) go through. *If* I can get through it, properly with no halfway houses, then that will surely give me enough self-esteem to last a lifetime.

It felt strange again going home this afternoon, and some damaging thoughts did arise, but it was good to see some friendly faces and to have the opportunity to make some positive choices. I'm still feeling a bit dodgy but I look even worse! I've come a long way in a short time but I've got a bit more to go and it's important that momentum is maintained. Putting my scales up in the loft is one small step, not irreversible, but it will help all the same. I still look terrible and I'm still tired, so there's still a distance to go. It was good, though, to feel as though I could help her in the way she has helped me—hope she appreciated the company at 2 a.m. I've got to keep this libido in check though!

Wednesday 20 January: Day 38

I'm not sure if I'm completely over Monday yet, and lots of old feelings are coming back—stand or sit? Long way round or short cut? To carry the bags or leave them for someone else?—from now on this is going to be hard. I know part of the appeal of my eating disorder is that I'm afraid to lose the protection it gives me. Obviously it is partly to do with weight, but Anorexia has also provided me with a convenient excuse. How could I be expected to amount to anything, academically, career-wise or in relationships, with this hanging over me? What if I stay in a dead-end job, don't find a partner, end up going back to my parents' house for my tea every day, would it be worth all the effort of fighting back? These fears are very real.

I know that my concept of what is "normal" is completely screwed and that is why I have to try to ignore the feelings I'm having. I've run out of answers and I just need to go with it. No, the staffs' jobs do not depend on my recovery, but I sense a measure of compassion amongst everyone here that I would be foolish not to utilise. I can do this but to get where I want to be I have to focus now. I have no more excuses, so just do it.

I knew Mum wouldn't want to go to Australia, although I wish she did, and at least I think she understands why it's something I have to do. Dad was also predictable, and I knew that his usual worries about money and my job would be swiftly followed by a comment about my weight. He clearly has no faith in my ability to recover but, you know what, why don't I just prove him wrong. Let's show him and give him something to be proud about. Amber is right, sending them a letter will make no difference. This will be a long-term thing and will take a lot of evidence and a lot of talking. It's little things like getting Mum to blitz my kitchen that will make a difference, not grand gestures. I've eroded our relationship bit by bit and that's the only way it can be restored. The way I speak about them sometimes it's as if they are the enemy, and there have been times when I have genuinely felt that to be true, but I can see now that the Anorexia is the enemy. Their love and support has never been enough for me to change, and it still is not, but it can be a bonus extra if I see this through to the end.

Thursday 21 January: Day 39

BMI: 17.2

The more often I say I'm fine and pleased with how things are going the more repetitive and less convincing it sounds. I think my decision to limit my exercise was a positive one, but I can also see Amber's point about not going to the extreme of denying myself completely, as this is unlikely to aid my recovery. Today's walk down to the beach was a happy medium. Groups are a bit dodgy at the moment. Whilst I want to get as much out of them as possible, and dearly want to help people, I am conscious of making empty gestures and of saying the wrong thing. Everyone is in their own private battle and I do not want to say anything that could be damaging or could make me look like an idiot. After every group now it seems as if I need to seek reassurance that I haven't put my foot in it, particularly with those I feel closest to, and I don't want to be seen as talking the talk before I have shown even the tiniest indication of being able to walk the walk. Is that a sign of the doubts that still exist within me about my own recovery? Probably.

LIVING THE DREAM

Everything seemed set up for me—my own house (rented, then a purchase after six months), a dream job in a lovely part of the world and my whole life in front of me. In time I would also come to value my new home's close proximity to the local eating disorders unit.

For the first few weeks I floated on a bubble of enthusiasm at having finally secured my job working in the sport that I had made my life. One of my first tasks was to count all the footballs in the store room! Anorexia wanted its bit of my new life too, of course, and I soon established a new exercise regime taking advantage of having my workplace practically on my doorstep. I put in an hour's walk before breakfast, before a five minute jog to and from work every morning, lunch time and evening, something which amused the local schoolchildren no end. Not even their taunts, though, were enough to deflect me from doing what I had to do to stay fit and to get fitter. As far as I was concerned my new colleagues knew nothing of my past and I was determined that would be how it should remain. If I did just enough to satisfy Anorexia, I could keep it reined in and stop the voice ever getting loud enough to drown everything else out again. I felt, *I knew*, I was back in control.

The walk before work, in particular, gave me a massive sense of my own superiority over everyone else, as I got my exercise quota in for the day before they had even woken up. I approached each walk in the same way I was living my life as an anorexic. Head down, non-stop until I had completed what I "had" to do, making sure I went round the outside of every corner, up and down every available step and curb, crossing the road at exactly the same point regardless of oncoming traffic or whether anyone was walking with me. As with the other aspects of my anorexic routine, every extra inch walked seemed so important, every deviation from the script so horrific to contemplate that everything else got pushed aside in the absolute necessity of doing "enough" every day. I would have liked to take the time to take in my surroundings, just as it would have been nice to occasionally slow down and savour the good parts of my life, but this was nowhere near as important as making sure that I had followed the plan and proved how healthy I was. So I kept going, through all weathers and ignoring any concerns that were voiced about my behaviours, head down through life refusing to change anything no matter how it affected those around me.

At work I soon established how much I could get away with, standing at all opportunities, walking up and down when opening letters or putting together leaflets and making up excuses to go upstairs where I could do press-ups and sit-ups to my heart's content. After work I would walk for an hour both before and after my evening meal, before finishing off my exercises and then 'allowing myself' to sit down for a couple of hours before bed, although even then only when eating. At various intervals I would cycle during my lunch break, taking food into work so that I could exercise in that spare hour. I began standing when eating at home, and would use any time alone in the office (my boss was a significant member of the F.A. and was often involved in high level meetings away from the county) to walk endlessly up and down—whilst attempting to do my job at the same time. These rituals soon had a serious impact on my job, and I only just survived my probationary period. Although I did rein in some of my behaviours over time, my relationship with my boss never really recovered, and I was extremely lucky to be able to leave the job on my own terms a couple of years down the line.

At the same time, my Anorexia was taking over the rest of my life to a greater and greater extent, and every calorie, every extra yard of walking was becoming ever more vitally important. As always, my parents were worried sick about me and they were soon expressing concern about my falling weight. The cold winters caused havoc with my feet and hands to the extent that it became painful to hold things, to write without blood marking the paper and even to go for a walk (not that it stopped me). One of my lowest moments and, I suspect, for my parents came when my Mum had to perform extensive first aid on my feet, which were red raw and cut from all the pressure they had had to bear.

This occurred during one of my parents' occasional visits to Dorset, every one of which I had come to dread to an ever-increasing degree. All I could think about in the weeks leading up to these occasions was how their presence would disrupt my routine, how they would be watching my every move and what steps I would have to take before and after their stay in order to compensate for the exercise lost and the inevitable, huge meal out that I would have to go through. And it was not just the prediction of calories added and miles not walked that filled me with foreboding, but also the sure fire knowledge that somewhere during our time together, the questions would arise: "Are you sure you're ok?", "You haven't been losing weight again, have you?", "If only you could eat a bit more it would make us really happy", to which the answers were always "Yes", "No" and "I'm really trying". I hated lying so much and I hate the wall that Anorexia put between my parents and me, but I feared even more the divide that I knew they would put between Anorexia and me. All I could do was smile when they arrived, count the hours and calories and walks until they left and then write them a letter apologising for my mood over the weekend and promising to try really hard to eat a bit more and to exercise a bit less, before doing all I could to placate my Anorexia and return to my anorexic life.

Nothing they said or did at this time could deflect me from my path, especially as I still retained the belief that I was ok. That's what I had been told when I was discharged from Leicester General Hospital and, while I recognised that my Anorexia had caused severe difficulties in my life and my work since that time, maybe that's what recovery meant for me. After all, I hadn't died or even been admitted to an eating disorders unit like those severe cases I'd read about and, while this wasn't how I had imagined "recovery" to be, I had been locked for so long into my anorexic mindset that I could see no way it would improve. In my mind I often envisaged a time when things would be different, when that switch would flick on and everything would be better, and thus to prepare myself for a time when I would be eating more and exercising less I had to do everything within my power to keep the situation from changing further. And so "Anorexic John" kept going, becoming more and more anorexic and moving further and further away from "John" with every step.

There have been very few moments over the last fifteen years in which I have imagined a halfway house between the absolutes of Anorexia and "fatness"; these to me were the only options available. Every mental recount of the sorry aspects of my existence—the pain, the tiredness, the lack of friends—were rounded off with the reassurance that "at least I'm not fat", with all the negative connotations and memories that that word held for me. To be faced with the very real belief that this is all your future can possibly amount to, either thinness and isolation or fatness and ridicule, does make it hard to summon up any enthusiasm for living, but something keeps you going, whether that be a tiny sliver of hope that things can change or just the ability to delude oneself that, actually, you do enjoy all the exercise and the independence and the nights alone, and anyway, at least you're not starving in Africa, at least you have control. It is amazing how much pain you can endure before your body gives up—one massive concern was that I might suffer an injury which would stop me exercising. On one occasion I fell off my bike into the path of a 4 X 4 which proceeded to drive over my arm. Somehow I escaped with just a deep cut, but the thought of going to hospital never crossed my mind. How could I explain to hospital staff that I couldn't possibly eat anything if they insisted on me lying in bed all day?

I'm not sure what it was that made me think that there could be more to a "Recovered Me", or whether it was just simply that my performance at work had become so compromised and my body so sore and so cold and so tired that Anorexia began to appear to not offer all the answers. My parents' continued show of support and desperate helplessness did, I think, have some effect in galvanising me into investigating whether there was something for me beyond "Anorexic John", but then that support had been a constant throughout my illness. As would be repeated later in my journey, it was only my own admittance that Anorexia had again taken over my life that opened the door to the help that was available. I confessed all to my boss, who much to my surprise (this was becoming a theme) did not seem at all shocked by the details of my secret, but given the frankly ludicrous behaviours I displayed in order to fulfil my exercise quota whilst at work, I can't believe that I thought she wouldn't know. The lengths I'd taken to avoid the staff Christmas meal, as well as my clearly compromised physical state were also obvious signs. With her backing, I went to my G.P., who referred me to the Kimmeridge Court Eating Disorders Unit. And so began the longest, toughest fight of my life.

9 July 2004

Dear John

Just a few words with the enclosed which your mother printed off the internet. We thought it could be useful for you to know that the website is available if you ever feel that it could be of help to you.

I know that it is only you that can take steps to gain weight and do not want to go on to you about it all the time, but it would make us both very happy if you could just put on a bit to reduce any risk to your health and future happiness, especially as you're enjoying your job so much and have a nice house. It would be a great shame to jeopardise any of this for the sake of a stone. I know you are trying your best, so please keep it up and hopefully put on a pound a week.

Hope you have a nice weekend. Take care and look after yourself.

Take care.
Mum & Dad

KIMMERIDGE COURT DIARY
WEEK 6

A bizarre week, possibly the pivotal week of my second inpatient admission and certainly a week which perfectly illustrates how my mood and belief system could change from day to day and even hour to hour. On the one hand I received a raft of compliments, from work colleagues who seemed genuinely pleased to see me for the first time since my admission and from fellow patients who I could see had no agenda and no reason to go out of their way in making me feel better about myself. In an artificial world such as Kimmeridge Court, it is often only the goodwill of others that keeps you going, as well as the "rewards" you accrue as you progress within the programme. This week also brought two such rewards—being allowed to leave support after half an hour and joining the Food Management group, and thus being permitted to inflict my cooking "skills" on everyone else.

In contrast to these definite positives, I also had to confront ever louder echoes of my Anorexia and, most abhorrent to me, accusations from another patient that I was bullying her. Given my own experiences, this really floored me and it was a struggle to harness my anger and use it in a positive way.

Friday 22 January: Day 40

My progress (*on the unit*) so far has manifested itself mainly in big gestures—not walking every day, going for larger portions, eating extra stuff—but it's not just those things that need to change. If I really am going to leave Anorexia behind then I am going to have to stop everything—weighing food, using crockery to measure, fishing for compliments, checking myself—and it's these behaviours that are going to be harder to shift. Amber's point about exercise has been on my mind a lot. How do I exercise for pleasure? It seems such an alien concept: how do I dip my toe into that ocean without drowning? The thing is, exercise is good and healthy, any doctor will tell you that, but exercising to excess, to schedule and to the exclusion of everything else is absolutely not healthy. Whilst my anorexic existence was limiting, so too would be a life in which I was afraid to exercise for fear of catching the bug again. If it's a nice day and I have an hour to kill, then I should be able to go for a walk. If the weather's crap or I have something more important to do then I should feel comfortable going without. How great will my life be if I can get to that point?

And how great would it be to respond to hunger like a "healthy" person? As time goes on more and more potential obstacles to recovery do seem to present themselves, and it is difficult to see how I can change the course of history and keep going without checking or weighing etc. Despite this, I still believe. I have no real basis for this, but something inside me looks upon recovery as something that will happen. I've just got to keep looking forward. PMA. Maintain your focus.

Good stuff—bargains; talking to Kym and Brian.

Saturday 23 January: Day 41

Encouraging visit to work. As expected everyone said I was looking "better" and, although my Anorexia is screaming "better" = "fatter", I have to say I agree with them: what's the point in denying reality? My worry is that they may think that everything is fine and that I should be back to work soon. I'm not so concerned that they will think I am "cured"—my battle will continue regardless—but that I will be pressured to return too quickly, leaving the work on my recovery half-completed like my first admission. Part of me would actually like to get back to work but I suspect that is the Anorexia talking. I am not ready.

This week has demonstrated to me how tough this is going to be. The old thoughts have definitely been more prominent, casting the first clouds over my sunny disposition. There seem to be so many little challenges within recovery that to fight every single one is going to take all the willpower and strength I have, or hope I have. Days like today should encourage me to keep going, but is that what I want, a life pretty much identical to before, with slightly more sitting down and less exercise? I've again shown how much I thrive on human contact, so why deprive myself of that or even the chance of some kind of relationship?

Sunday 24 January: Day 42

The anorexic mind does not allow much space for sense to invade its territory, but if you can take a step back, it is possible to counter its argument. Eating that shortcake (fat, calories, my choice) today was "wrong" on so many levels (eating outside meals = extra exercise to compensate). When I thought about it though, about all the hundreds of organs, vessels and cells that all have to take their bit of energy from it, it's unlikely that much is left over to develop into fat. Amidst all the positivity and the "you're looking better", it's sometimes difficult to remember that I'm still UNDERWEIGHT, and that five/six weeks more in hospital could yet be an underestimation. Six weeks in and I've no complaints so far, but the hard work is still to come and I've yet to achieve anything new or substantial. I have to keep going. PMA. Forward not back.

> Good stuff—Scrabble with Abbie, talk with Emily, snack out, talk with Hannah, talk with Mum and Dad.

Monday 25 January: Day 43

BMI: 17.4

I'm now entering territory unchartered over the last three years but my weight is less now a question of numbers and is based more on how I feel, day to day. Without access to scales I know that this is my only real way of checking myself, and trying to limit my ways of doing that has been as tough as anything. I can see the logic behind it though (*not weighing myself*), as I can never hope to truly break through unless my obsession with weight and how I look is battled through. As with my first admission, the physical stuff is (relatively) easy; getting through to my brain is something else entirely.

Today has been instructive. The times over the last six weeks when I have been most anxious, most vulnerable to my anorexic voice is when I'm upset, be it a weight issue or something that makes me angry, such as today (*being accused of bullying by another patient*). What is clear though is that using these accusations will not act as motivation for me. Nothing, not my family's pain, my cocked-up career, my inability to run and play football, my lack of a social life or intimate relationship, the way I have treated Hannah, none of it has worked before, and neither will this, recovery will only come from within me, from my own motivation, my own desire to claim a better future for myself. When I can look back on my Anorexia, I will see days like today as just that, days, moments in my life which can be filed away with all the crap, good and indifferent days that will make up the rest of my life. This anger from today will only last six weeks, and then I can leave it far behind in my past. She's not worth it. You are.

> Good stuff—Scrabble with Abbie, talk with Hannah (again), talk with Dr. Macken, time away from unit (to clear my head), only having to do half an hour's support.

Tuesday 26 January: Day 44

Well that felt good, and you know what, I could actually take that in. Neither Margot nor Abbie have any agenda, any reason to suddenly label me an "inspiration", and that is worth a thousand times more than anything I may hear from my family or the staff. I've sat there in group after group saying that this is the real me, how I was before Anorexia entered my life, and that any praise I receive is for who I am, not what I am or how I look. The key to recovery, and what I failed to remember last time, is how I translate that to a year from now, to the outside world, where there is no-one to massage my ego. Hannah's friendship will obviously be important, as she makes me feel so good, but it would be completely unfair to rely on her alone. Is the praise of people here enough to sustain me through all the bad times, the criticism and the weight gain? I don't know, but I owe it to Margot and Abbie to take the risk of finding out.

Surely to goodness I need no more motivation than today. Being described as an "inspiration" was humbling and, uniquely, I felt open to it. No strings, just two young women, with their own problems, giving me genuine praise for being me; not anorexic, hard-working, head-down John, but just for being John. I'm also clearly someone whom people believe they can trust—the evidence I crave is all there before me again. The trick is whether I can remember days like these in the down times. I'm definitely noticing physical differences now and it is becoming harder to resist checking and flexing. The difficult work starts here, but at this moment, the future doesn't scare me, it excites me. There are a hundred million things that can go wrong, but what if they don't . . . . PMA. Forward not back. To the future.

Good stuff—Talks with Stan and Davina. Chat with Hannah and
Kym. Scrabble with Abbie. Five minute ego trip. Just a great day.

Wednesday 27 January: Day 45

Definitely feeling more anxious this morning. I'm trying hard not to
look in the mirror, not to stare at my face as my cheeks seem to expand in
front of my eyes, or to compare my legs as they are now to the sixteen year
old legs that have supported me for the last fourteen years. I can deal with
the idea of the numbers going up, of approaching a healthy BMI, but every
second of the day I am encountering new feelings and all parts of my body
appear to be getting larger every day. Since I started here I've gone up a belt
size, my clothes hang better, my backside doesn't hurt when I sit down and,
while I can see the positive in all of this, it is also frightening because these
physical changes are what everyone notices. Nothing is going to stop me
reaching BMI 20, and I remain excited by the possibilities that lie in front
of me, but these feelings will haunt me for the immediate future, and I still
need support to keep them at bay.

As I see it, I'm going to BMI 20. In the mean time I am going to feel
fat, bloated, out of control and be severely tempted to run out the door and
give in to voice that commands my existence. But you know what, that life
offers nothing to me anymore. Besides not being fat, I can't think of one
single benefit it gives me. Ok, it will leave me "exposed", but I can hardly
be any worse in my job, my relationships, my family life. Lord only knows
what the future will hold, but that's the point, a future without Anorexia
has no boundaries, no deadlines or schedules. Life is there to be grabbed.

Tonight was fantastic (*pub quiz with Robyn to celebrate her leaving the
unit tomorrow*), and just as life should be: two friends, out for a drink with
no hang-ups, no hurry and no need to walk home. More kind words—and
finally I feel ready to accept them. I've got a feeling Robyn will be ok,
she seems to be aware of the need to look forward and to have a support
network in place. It's people like her who don't deserve this—and neither
do I—and I owe it to her and to everyone here to fight until my last breath
to beat this. I hope and don't believe that will be necessary. PMA. Forward
not back. Keep the pressure on.

Good stuff—Food management for first time, Scrabble with Abbie,
Pub Quiz, Kind words. Keep going.

Thursday 28 January: Day 46

BMI: 17.6

Another kilo this week—things progressing as planned. The anxious feelings brought on by physical changes are becoming more frequent and will not go away for the foreseeable future. I have to forget any notion of BMI 18 being "healthy", as BMI 20 is my target, regardless of how I feel. Until I reach that point I will only be a part person, and I deserve to be whole again, with no trace of this nightmare remaining. The only chance of that happening is to keep going, reach maintenance and take a chance—only then can I prove that this is the time. It holds nothing for me.

Family Matters group left me with a lot to think about, and again confirmed to me how lucky I have been. My relationship with my parents has not been great since Anorexia entered our lives, and there is still a lot of work to be done to rebuild those bridges. Nothing they have said or done, however, can be blamed for my situation, even though they themselves have probably searched endlessly for a cause. What I am sure of is that there is no point regretting what has gone before, as I can never begin to repair the damage my Anorexia has done. All I can do is look towards being a good son in the future, and to do that I need to keep my focus. Like Robyn says, it is, and I am, worth it.

JOHN'S ANOREXIC MINDSET

I'm ok.

I mean, I always say "I'm ok" because any hint of vulnerability will have them round here before I finish speaking, forcing me to eat and not allowing me to live my life.

I'm ok.

Yeah, yeah, I know what I'm missing out on—I can't run, jump, concentrate, get on with my parents, go out with my friends, eat anything cooked by other people, eat when I don't exercise, do my job properly, play football—but, you see, none of that matters because I have Anorexia and it protects me and keeps me thin and won't allow them to pick on me.

People say I need some flesh on me and them saying that lifts me ten feet high, knowing that I look thinner than other people. My family say I've got to eat, but they would say that, it's their job. Everything I eat is ultimately down to me, and I'm the one who has to deal with the guilt, the constant nagging in my head until I have exercised it out. I can't deal with putting on weight, as to accept one extra gram will be to let my willpower go and my weight will balloon out of control.

This is the only thing I'm good at, the only thing that makes me stand out.

I can't beat it, so I have to deal with it.

I get such a buzz being there when other people eat, stuffing their mouths on the sofa while I sit there with my diet lemonade. Every time I resist, every time I ignore the rumble of my stomach, or go that extra mile when my legs are tired, it's another day of not being fat, another day of safe, secure, no-risk. When everything else is going to ruins I can just touch my ribs and everything is ok again.

Being an anorexic means that I am someone.

I stand out as someone with willpower, determination, in control. I know how much I love food so I have to be extra vigilant. I have to keep checking that people can see my thinness, I need that reassurance. As long as I do everything, anything to keep my weight from going up it will all be ok. I have to work harder because of my fat body; other people can eat junk and lounge around and stay slim and don't care, but if I let my guard drop for a second I will lose everything and I will be the fat, lazy slob that everyone knows I am.

I wish things were different, I really do but Anorexia will never leave me and therefore I have to live with it and the consequences it will have for my life. Other people live alone, don't have kids, don't go out and at least Anorexia gives me the excuse not to do those things. And it's because Anorexia keeps me from succeeding elsewhere that I have to keep it with me, because at least people can see that I am a successful anorexic.

Looking at other people fascinates me. How can they be happy being so fat? It makes me feel so good to be thinner than they are. How much food must those gym bunnies have to eat to be so muscular? I do sometimes wish I was like them, but they must have to eat loads so it wouldn't be worth the risk. It's great when I see a fat person, guessing how many of me you could fit into one of them. Their lack of willpower just makes me feel so superior, so much more in control. I remember when I used to enjoy eating, when I used to look forward to meals, it seems like another world. I never felt superior then. I was sad then, not like now. I keep telling them that I'm happy, but they say they can't understand how I can be.

I just want them to understand.

I just want them to leave me alone.

They want to know why I have to be thin, why I don't want to go out, why I have to go for a walk, and all I can do is say 'I'm fine', 'I'm not losing weight', 'Why don't you trust me?'. I have to keep Anorexia close, or else they will try to take it away, making me fat by keeping me prisoner and force feeding me. If I talk about it to people it's like I want their help, but I don't need their help, I just need some space to live my life. They know I'm seeing someone about it, why isn't that enough? I never wanted this, but they don't get it, they think I'm punishing them for something. Surely they can see that by keeping it private, keeping them out I'm protecting them too. I was such a goody two shoes, such a 'sensible boy' that to see their son with a mental illness must be crushing. If I told them everything it would only cause them to worry more and probably come down here to 'look after me'. That must never happen. I want to beat this, I will beat this, but in my own way and when I'm ready.

They know that I'm a failure and if it wasn't for this I would amount to nothing.

That is the reason behind everything, the diets, the exercise, the arguments and all the nights home alone. I need them because Anorexia needs them and he gives me what I am incapable of giving myself—respect.

KIMMERIDGE COURT DIARY
WEEK 7

This week began with a significant milestone in the stay of any Kimmeridge Court resident—the first weekend leave. It shows that you are being trusted to follow the programme yourself, that you have progressed and also acts as the first real sign that the end of your stay is in sight. I was determined that I must not let this "freedom" deflect my progress, so agreed with Abbie that I should challenge myself every weekend to have a takeaway, and to report back as soon as the deed was done. Proper facing fear time!

Back at Kimmeridge, however, I was finding it difficult to believe that all my new friendships were entirely genuine and my Anorexia was really kicking in, trying to convince me that they all secretly hated me. This anxiety, however, was nothing compared to that which greeted me once I stepped on the scales.

Friday 29 January: Day 47

Just seen another man, probably mid-20s, and instantly felt like crossing the road, as if he would take one look at me and laugh. A part of me still regards this all as a shameful episode, that having this "girl's illness" makes me something of a lesser man. I always recite the line about how this is nothing to be ashamed of, of how we can do nothing to prevent it and how there are probably a lot more male sufferers out there. What is it about me, though, that meant that I didn't hide it away, I didn't adopt a stiff upper lip and "be a man about it"? I reached a point where I could go no further alone and cried—literally—for help. I don't regard myself as a wimp or a coward for this, in fact I think it is the bravest thing I have ever done, to concede my inability to fight this alone, especially second time around where the feelings of failure and having let people down were even more pronounced. Something remains, however, maybe a fear of other people's reactions, maybe the bullies are still winning. Then again, if I remain fearful of being bullied for being both overweight and underweight, then I suppose the obvious solution is to maintain at a healthy weight!

I've always known that recovery would be a long-term thing, that once I'd repeated my restoration to BMI 20 that the really hard work of maintaining that level would have to begin, as well as addressing the issues underlying my Anorexia. This part has always been easy in comparison. The removal of guilt, the desire to please and the general therapeutic environment mean that I can put weight on while I'm here. The far harder task will be to sustain this momentum in the real world, where I am not being praised constantly for my progress or surrounded by positive people, but where all my flaws, real or imagined, are suddenly laid bare.

Saturday 30 January: Day 48

Phase one of weekend leave successfully completed—Cod, chips and mushy peas, no questions asked, no compensatory behaviour, although anxious feelings were definitely enhanced and the desire to check myself was also heightened. However, I did it (despite the cost) and that at least is something, even if there remains a marked difference between my attitude during Weight Restoration and Maintenance. One failure, though, I did look at the calorie content of my cooking oil—I must resist this. On the other hand, I have bought some non-diet squash, and drunk some of it too!

Things are tougher here, away from the unit with its rules and staff watching over you. Mostly though, I feel very lonely here. Despite the occasional tensions, I feel very much at home at Kimmeridge Court—again—and I have thrived on the company of so many caring, friendly individuals. It is their struggle, and the enjoyment I have got from being around them, that fuels my belief that there is more to life than Anorexia. In this moment, I struggle to see what it holds for me.

Why should I be surprised that this is tough? Seven weeks is never going to be enough to eradicate fourteen years of pain. I don't want to belittle what I have achieved so far but it is too reminiscent of my last admission for me to get overexcited. I think this time will be different, but I have no real evidence. At the moment I am all talk, no trousers. Still, new beginnings.

PMA. Look forward, not back.

Sunday 31 January: Day 49

Well, I survived my first night home alone, although it is more a sense of having got through it rather than feeling as though I have achieved anything significant. The calorie counting was a warning sign and, whilst I didn't do anything stupid, the biggest thing in my head is that I still haven't proved anything. As I approach a healthy weight, I'm getting images of how that will actually be for me. I guess I still look upon "fit" as being "not fat", by which I mean no fat at all—skinny or muscular, with no wobbly bits. At BMI 20 I probably will see some fat, at least in my mind's eye, and that will be hard to get my head around. It's so difficult to block out memories of how I looked and felt when checking myself, and curbing that will be one of the hardest steps on the road to recovery.

I still believe.

Monday 1 February: Day 50

BMI: 17.8

50 days in and I've reached the big 50. 50 kg is a mark that would have seemed unimaginable before Christmas, and it just goes to prove that it never was about numbers: a 0.1 kg rise would have been just as bad as a 1 kg increase, it was just the knowledge that it had occurred under my own watch. The big question is would things be any different now? If, when faced with a fall in my weight, would I have it in me to reverse the decline? I never have before and I have major doubts as to whether I will be able to react positively when faced with that situation. Again, it raises the question of "what is recovery?" Is it simply regaining and maintaining a healthy body shape and weight, of which I consider myself capable, or is it reaching a point where food and weight become side issues to life and in which I accept the vicissitudes of weight as being of little concern. To achieve the latter will be extremely difficult and may be beyond my capability.

The more time I spend here, the more I hear of the pain and suffering in the lives of bright, beautiful women who have been cursed by this illness, the more I just want to leave it behind. It pains me to think of the wasted years, the ruined and never-were relationships and the opportunities I've missed, but then there is nothing I can do about that now. The Anorexia continues to whisper from the sidelines—*greedy, fat, out of control, dislikeable, hypocrite, they're only pretending to like you*—and while I haven't reacted negatively to this, the voice remains and could get stronger. I suppose it comes back to risk, and whether I want to live a life devoid of all risk or whether I gamble for something better. Part of that gamble will be to voice my belief in myself and my recovery. It sounds corny and I will be setting myself up for a massive fall, but if that belief is reinforced through saying it then I should do it.

Tuesday 2 February: Day 51

Dodgy morning, with plenty of reminders about how far I have to go. I still struggle to believe that people will like me for who I am or that the evidence I have that they do is genuine. My Anorexia screams at me that they really hate me, that they're just being polite, and it's those feelings, rather than the concerns about food and exercise that I really have to overcome if I am going to fully recover.

The same is true with my remark about the staff singing (*very badly*). It was a spontaneous joke, but as soon as I said it the negative thoughts came to mind—*does anyone else think it's funny? Do I sound rude? Do the staff think I'm stupid? The staff say I'm ok but what do they really think?* Then the feelings of fatness spring forward and things in life and on the unit that I can normally deal with suddenly appear that much more insurmountable.

Recovery will happen, but I have to work really hard for the next year. That has to take priority over everything, including finance and work. My recovery has to be everything, and improving my family and social life will be a major component in this. Unless I can convince myself that there is more to me than this illness—hell, that there is anything to "John" at all—then all this work will again go to waste. Cards on the table time. There is now too much riding on this to keep going half-hearted. I don't want to go to Australia as a compromised boy living a compromised life and have a compromised holiday. If I don't believe in my ability to recover then I should quit right now and go back to my half life. By staying I am committing to the future, which means doing exactly as I am told, forgetting the past, all the rules and beliefs that have come to shape my existence. I have to bear the crap times and the moments my Anorexia tells me that I am crap, because I have so much evidence now that that isn't the case, and what is relevant now, today, will still be relevant in ten, fifteen years' time. I have no idea what a "recovered" me is capable of or, frankly, how I'm going to get there, and Australia is incidental in the great scheme of things, but if I want to stop regretting my life and start to live it then I have to take a step into the darkness.

One thing I do know is that I do trust the staff here implicitly. They believe in me, the other patients believe in me, so it's about time I did too. Yes Australia is incidental, but it's also symbolic. I won't recover because of Australia, for the same reason I haven't recovered due to my family, my job, my life. I will recover because *I* want to, because I have the support and because I BELIEVE.

Wednesday 3 February: Day 52

The closer I get to my 30th birthday, the more it is dawning on me how much of my life I have wasted. I've had no girlfriends, rubbish jobs, few friends, no real family life and here I am, about to spend my birthday in hospital again. This has to stop, and I have to keep challenging myself. That's why I had the Steak & Ale pie in the pub today, not to impress anyone—not that they would care—but because if I continue to deny myself then my Anorexia will survive. I have to try and eradicate every trace of the illness if I want to leave it behind, and that's why this will be a long, tough job, with many setbacks.

Thursday 4 February: Day 53

BMI: 18.5

SHIT! That weight was unexpected and right now I don't know what to think. I have been feeling that my head was racing ahead of my body, but it appears as if my body is ready to overtake. To be honest, my initial reaction—other than gobsmacked surprise—was one of satisfaction. At least there was a reason for my feeling "bigger". What does it mean now though? No pub meals, no snacks at all? I've been having slightly larger portions but I'm a bloke and it seemed a really positive thing. I've done nothing out of the ordinary to cause this and it's put my head in a spin. I still need to keep trusting what I am being told, though, or my whole recovery doesn't amount to anything. This is an anomaly, but at least it might accelerate things. I just don't want them (*the staff*) to think I've been going outside the programme, as their trust in me is really important. My Anorexia is screaming at me—"*see, you are a fat man who will keep on putting on weight, you can't control this, you eat too much, you're lazy"*—but I *don't* believe it.

I've been thinking a lot about how the competition with my best friend affected my self-esteem when I was young, and how it still affects me now. I was jealous of him, of his house and all his toys but I spent so much time there it was almost a second home anyway. We spent loads of time together when we were young boys before branching into separate interests—him into guitar playing and scouts where he was constantly graded and praised and me into playing football, usually on my own, where no amount of practice seemed to elicit any improvement. I haven't spoken to him for twelve years, but still something goes off in the back of my mind every time my Mum says about how well he's doing in America. To be honest, I think this is now less to do with comparing myself to him and more with regards to my own disappointment with how my life has gone, but I definitely felt that competition when I was younger.

Well, I got through the day and, even though I've lost my evening pudding (I can't believe I'm complaining!), I'm still on course. I've lost all faith in my ability both to check myself and to predict what will happen on the scales. All I can do is go with it and put all my trust in the staff here. I believe I will get better and the only way I can see me reaching recovery is to put my faith in what I am being told. My Anorexia is screaming at me but I'm too tired to fight anymore. I just want to move on.

REACHING ROCK BOTTOM

6 January 2005

Dear John

As promised I am enclosing 100 bags for your Star Wars figures. You can keep the other bags for me to use if you can't find a use for them.

We are really pleased that you have such a positive attitude since seeing the Doctor on Tuesday and know that you will get "there" this time. It must be reassuring for you to know that so many people are rooting for you. Just like Everton who were quite low down the league last season, we know you will make a good comeback.

Thank you for entertaining us last weekend, we are looking forward to seeing you next month. Look after yourself.

Mum

It came as a massive relief to be able to give up the pretence of my "recovery", regardless of the hit to my self-esteem that conceding defeat in my battle with Anorexia undoubtedly brought with it. I felt sure that this time everything would be different and resolved to do all I could to use my weekly outpatient appointments to help me to crack it once and for all. Mercifully, considering the haphazard distribution of Eating Disorders units in other areas, Kimmeridge Court was only a couple of miles from my home, which meant I could take half-days from work and cycle to the bus station.

The possibility of an inpatient admission was raised at the first appointment with my therapist, although I was half expecting her to take one look at me and say I didn't have a problem! As far as I was concerned, inpatient admission was an impossibility as, although my employers were very understanding and helpful about my attending my weekly appointments, I could not see them being so willing to keep my job alive whilst I recovered, especially as I had made no mention of it during my job interview. In any case, I remained convinced recovery was achievable under my own volition.

Thus began nine months of determined talk of being ready to change and to do what was necessary, during which my weight never changed from the 40kg mark that had been constant since I left Manchester. I would assure my therapist that I was really committed while never revealing the full extent of my exercise regime, especially not the fact that I always got off one bus stop early to jog the rest of the way to my appointments. Every suggestion she made, even the smallest of increases, seemed both so simple and yet so, so difficult to go through with and I just could not escape the cycle of guilt, exercise and solitude that had become my life. My ideas of less exercise and more food were to walk rather than jog and to not throw away half my packet of Ready Salted crisps because it contained 2 more calories than the other flavours. The changes I felt comfortable making weren't even baby steps when my battle with the illness required giant strides.

My performance at work was continuing to decline and my boss raised concerns that my health was becoming a real issue. In July 2005 it definitely did become a real issue, when I received the results of a bone scan the Doctor at Kimmeridge Court had arranged for me. The letter said I had osteoporosis in my spine, for which the only known solution would be prescribed medication and a return to a healthy weight. For a moment, I was taken away from my Anorexia and permitted to stare the reality of my situation full in the face. *Surely now*, with the shame of being told I had an old person's illness at the age of 25 and knowing that I would be popping pills on a daily basis, *surely* this was going to be "the thing" that would force me to change. This wasn't messing around anymore, this wasn't craving attention and I wasn't one of those anorexics in my book who came out the other side mentally but not physically scarred by the experience. How could I have been so stupid?

Not even this, however, could force itself into my thoughts ahead of the fear and the guilt that continued to stalk my mind every second of the day. I would wake with every good intention, every determination to use this proper, genuine disability as the ultimate incentive to change, but when it came to eating more or exercising less, the very moment of truth, I had neither the strength nor the will to change. My osteoporosis became another badge of honour to parade in front of anyone who doubted my success as an Anorexic, although there could be few of those. As usual, I kept my new-found condition from my parents, as this would only bring them more into my life and threaten my cherished independence.

I kept on keeping on, continually assuring people that I was really trying while offering no evidence of my willingness to fight, but eventually I had to admit that my therapist was right—I had stopped living a long time ago and had merely been "existing", maintaining an endless daily grind with the sole aim of not putting on weight. Some element of hope remained inside me but I knew that I couldn't do whatever it was I had to do alone.

When I suggested that my opposition to inpatient admission was wavering, events moved very quickly. I was given a brief tour of the inpatient unit (I thought the girls there all looked very ill, much worse than I was) and a place was made available as soon as my employer agreed to allow me twelve weeks' sick leave. On 11 October 2005 I began my first, and as far as I was concerned, only inpatient admission at Kimmeridge Court. I think my parents were relieved and I shared their conviction that this really would make a difference. On my first night I looked at my emaciated body in the mirror, and reality did begin to sink in. I stood there, looking straight into the reflection of my eyes, thinking over all the dreams I'd had and chances I'd missed. I looked terrible and I felt ashamed. The following morning, my weight had plummeted to BMI 12.8, only just above the threshold for bed rest and the prospect of being pushed in a wheelchair. I could not see how I could possibly go any lower than this.

KIMMERIDGE COURT DIARY
WEEK 8

A big week as I reach the end of my twenties, and become a proper grown-up. Except in my head I don't feel thirty, and I certainly haven't lived the life of a thirty year-old. Any thoughts of my impending old age were, in any case, put to one side as the thought of spending my birthday weekend with my parents brought my Anorexia back to the forefront of my consciousness with a vengeance. If it wasn't for their constant love and support I suspect Anorexia would have claimed me years ago, and yet there is no doubt that its strength is magnified when I am with them. Not a great weekend, but as usual seeing Hannah and my friends at Kimmeridge Court soon raised my spirits.

When I asked to be referred back to Kimmeridge Court, I felt that I needed a new perspective on my illness, having pretty much exhausted the patience and advice of my therapist during and after my first admission. This time I was assigned to Dr. Macken who I felt, as a man, could offer me that new perspective. We were spending a lot of time focusing on the subject of my primary school teacher asking me to write the names of disruptive classmates on the blackboard, and the consequences this has had for my life since then.

Friday 5 February: Day 54

Another good session with Dr. Macken. What would I tell my eight-year-old self if I could speak to him now? Lose some weight, probably! It's weird, and frightening, how little moments 20 years in the past can affect your whole life, but it demonstrates how fragile human existence is. Does it help me now to focus all my anger on my teacher for asking me to write the names on the board? Probably not, but to be honest the more I think about it the less I can summon up any real hostility. The whys and wherefores of why I'm spending the last days of my twenties in hospital have been gone over so many times that to keep using them as a focus for regret and anger seems increasingly futile, and can only keep me pinned back in the illness. It would be wrong to say that I don't care, this is my life after all, but I've spent fourteen years getting angry with the world whilst it has continued around me. I think it's time to move on.

I'm still apprehensive about spending the weekend with my parents, and I don't really know why. I guess I've spent so long fearing these weekends and pushing my parents away that the idea of actually "spending time" with them seems very alien. It's not as if I'm going to miss out on anything with them being here, but something about their presence takes me back to being "Anorexic John". I guess this is just another one of those risks I have to take.

My Anorexia is definitely stronger at home and particularly with my parents here. Nothing personal, but things feel so claustrophobic and I know it's going to take a long time before they trust me and I feel 100% comfortable in their presence. Still, there's only one way to do that and I have to keep fighting. Tonight has again proved that I have really, really good friends, in Wales, in Poole and at Kimmeridge Court and I have to stop taking them for granted. I don't feel fat, I don't really want to exercise, but something feels uneasy, and it's not the fact that I've just turned 30. If I didn't feel so inexperienced and hadn't missed out on so much then I don't think my age would bother me. Ah well, here's to the next 30 years.

> *Happy Birthday Mate. Hope it's a good one. Keir x*
> *That kiss was an accident but as it's your birthday tomorrow . . .*
> *Fuck it xxxxxxxxxxxxxxxxxxxxxxxxx men don't express their emotions enough*

Saturday 6 February: Day 55

So this is 30, and I'm coming to realise how tough this year will be. The simple truth is that in the "real world", away from the support of everyone at Kimmeridge Court—where anything seems possible—there are a huge number of challenges. I haven't been this weight at home for a long, long time and it feels much more uncomfortable than in the unit. My normal defence mechanism is to run away, and the urge to do so does seem stronger. My Anorexia is screaming at me in a way it hasn't for a while, even last week, and obviously being with my parents and all the memories that entails is a huge factor in this. I suddenly feel more sensitive to comments and eating with them.

This is the worst I've felt since my admission began. I don't think food and exercise is necessarily the issue but I feel so claustrophobic that I just want to be alone. Although both meals were large I have managed them, and even when my parents didn't clear their plates I did clear mine, but more and more as the night has dragged on, I've had unhelpful thoughts regarding my body shape and size and the food I've eaten. I'm finding it a lot harder tonight to take a step back and rationalise my thoughts. I really thought I was onto something but if I find it so difficult to be around my parents with their rumbling stomachs, the two greatest people in my life, what does that say about the state of my mind?

I just want to be alone.

Sunday 7 February: Day 56

God I feel like such a tosser. My parents are the best people in the world and yet I feel so uneasy around them. Whereas in Kimmeridge Court I can leave my past behind me it smacks me straight in the face whenever I'm with them and I always end up feeling crap for not being the son they deserve. How can I stand there and keep taking money off them when I have given them nothing in return? I still believe the future can be bright but it will be a long struggle, as this weekend has demonstrated, and I don't feel as if I can take on even more guilt at the moment. Things have been so forward-looking and so positive that this weekend has been a bit of a shock to the system. I can be all happy-happy and really confident but my Anorexia is always there, telling me I'm fat, telling me to leave food and to skip meals and to walk a bit further and to get away from anyone who gives a toss. Things like other people not clearing their plate or suggesting even the merest criticism shouldn't still affect me but they do and they stir up so many feelings that I am trying so hard to suppress. I wish it would all go away.

The truth is it's been so long since I spent any time with my parents as a healthy son that I don't know how to relate to them or to react to their presence in any way other than with suspicion and anxiety. I'm so used to imagining their eyes on me all the time and nitpicking that any suggestion of criticism gets my guard up. With my parents, all the lies, the anger, the tension, the guilt get thrown into the mix leaving me on edge even before they turn up. I'd been thinking that my weight was lagging behind my mind, so this weekend has been timely. Clearly I have a way to go still.

My belief has not been shaken—reinforced if anything—but the path to recovery is clearly going to be rocky.

Monday 8 February: Day 57

BMI: 18.4

Didn't expect my weight to go down, and not sure if I feel exhilarated or indifferent. I want to maintain the momentum but I've reached the point whereby I have no idea what the scales will show, so I am neither worried nor pleased about it. I'm just letting Kimmeridge Court take over—my fight has left me.

The more and more I talk about it and go on about my plans the less convincing I sound to myself and, probably, to others. The reminders of four years ago (*first "recovery"*) are screaming louder and louder each time I try to think of stuff to do other than the exercise that has dominated my life. Will I honestly find something else to do than walk?

(*After meeting Hannah*) *That* is why I have to keep fighting. There are people out there who do like me, who do care for me and don't care about my illness or the mistakes I've made or even the successes I've had. Hannah is someone who makes me feel good and who makes me feel as if this is all possible. The future is a huge unknown, but that is a massive step up from seeing nothing but Anorexia in front of me. I can be so much more just as a person, let alone anything else that to let all this go again would be cruel on other people, not just myself. I have a contribution to make, but I can only do that if healthy. Let's just do it.

Tuesday 9 February: Day 58

The battle to block out the voice is now getting really hard. Every time I look at my face, my stomach, my legs, my first thought is how much bigger they are. At the moment this is only a momentary thought and I can rationalise it—I've put on ten kg, I'm still underweight—but because I'm generally feeling unsure about myself I'm feeling less confident physically. There are loads of good things happening at the moment—Australia, Hannah, the staff here, the patients here, the thought of recovery—but then doubts: do they really like me?; what if I say the wrong things to staff or patients?; remember I've failed before; they are all coalescing at the moment to suppress my mood. I have no strategies to fall back on other than ones that have failed in the past. All I can do is ride it out, trust in what I am being told and hope that as I progress in the real world that things will improve and the voice will lessen.

Recovery certainly isn't going to be all bells and whistles. The number of obstacles that I can see, let alone those yet to reveal themselves, could overwhelm me, but at least there does appear to be a path there to negotiate. I may not reach Utopia, but anything has to be better than this. I'm not fat, in fact I still look ill. If I can get to a place where I am comfortable at a healthy weight and not thinking every day and every second of my body and food, then that will be 1000 per cent better than what I had before. And if I can make that level, and maintain it, then other goals will seem more attainable.

I think one of the keys to my recovery will be to accept that not everything I do has to be rated, praised or criticised. If I can never do anything or feel good about doing it without having that affirmation—if I can't do something for enjoyment's sake—then I will never move on, never find that key to my self-esteem with which to replace Anorexia. If I believe that I only do kind things to gain approval, then I will never escape the spiral of guilt that has kept me pinned down for too long. How would I react if someone told me that this book was a crap idea? Would I stop? Would I start to write it but never finish because that one voice kept nagging away? Sounds bloody stupid when I say it like that.

I'm still struggling to look people in the eye when I talk about recovery. Why is this? Is it because I don't believe? Is it because every time I do, I get flashbacks of old promises and failures? I don't know, but to worry about it seems futile. If I cock up again then, hey, at least I tried and didn't die wondering.

Wednesday 10 February: Day 59

I've never looked at it in this way before, but I have absolutely no concept of what a BMI 18 or 20 body looks like. To my eyes I am fat, or at least fatter than I was before, but everything else, the staff, the scales, the text books, tell me that I'm underweight. Am I arrogant enough to believe that I'm right and they're wrong? This must be what a BMI 18 body looks like, and a BMI 20 body will just about look healthy, and far nearer thin than fat. I might not like how a BMI 18, 19 or 20 body looks and feels, but if that is what it is then I can accept it. Maybe, just maybe, I'm wrong and

I'm not actually different from everyone else. Maybe everyone at BMI 18, of my sex, age, build, height etc, has a body like mine. What's the point of fighting nature?

Thursday 11 February: Day 60

BMI: 18.5

Although it's disappointing to have lost a little momentum, this week has been instructive. I'm now close to eating a "normal" diet and my weight has hardly moved, despite my limited exercise levels. I would feel guilty about my weight loss over the weekend if I felt I had done anything to affect it in a negative way, but I'm blowed if I can think of anything. As I've said before, all I can do is do what I'm asked and let my weight sort itself out. I'm more and more confident that I can get a handle on my weight. By far the greatest challenge will be tackling the demons in my head that existed long before Anorexia became the solution to my life.

A really good example of my problem has arisen this morning. Kym has had my leaving present since last night, and I have had no acknowledgement. Does this mean she hasn't seen it? Has she seen it but not liked it? Why am I so anxious to be thanked? Why am I expecting anything? Is my motive behind buying it merely getting praise in return? Do I need that gratitude to feel good about myself? What happens if she leaves without saying anything—will it ruin my day/weekend/life? If she says nothing, does that automatically mean that she doesn't like it? Am I comfortable taking that risk?

How do I function with a brain like this?!?!

THE NIGHTMARE BEFORE
CHRISTMAS 1998

Scene: Christmas Meal, December 1998, Beaumont Hall of Residence, Leicester University. John is sat with his friends as the kitchen staff start dishing out the food.

This is wrong.

I shouldn't be here, in this room, with all these people so happy and chatty and not caring about the huge amount of food we are about to eat. I've done so well not to lose any more weight, that's what Dr Brown said. "Eat little and often, little and often". Well this isn't going to be anywhere near little, this is going to be huge and disgusting and I will be huge and disgusting after eating it. I was doing so well, just keeping my weight steady until I see the therapist Dr. Brown was talking about, no need to go too fast yet and I will put on weight after Christmas, I promised I would, but I'm not ready yet.

This feels so wrong. I can't believe they persuaded me to come.

Tom *"It's the Hall Christmas meal, you've got to go, everyone else is going"*
John *"Thanks for asking and I'd really love to go but I don't think I can, I've got loads of work to do"*

> **John's Anorexia** *"That's it, any excuse, anything to get them to go away and leave you to your exercise and YOUR food. You've fobbed them off easily before, and you do have work to do. It'll be too late to walk up the gym afterwards too and you wouldn't have enough time to do all the exercise you'd need to do to compensate for eating too much. That's too much disruption. Best not go and mess our evening up. Think of all that food, all that sitting down, all those eyes looking at you and how greedy you are. There's not even any choice over what you eat and I can't feign vegetarianism now. No, best just to stay here".*

Tom *"Rubbish, I'm not taking no for an answer. You have to go; it'll look weird if you don't. You won't have to eat much . . ."*

John *"No, I know and I'd really like to come but I have so much to do and I have to ring my parents and have a shower and really I can't . . . ."*

John's Anorexia *"This is not working you idiot. You are so weak it's unbelievable. Think of something, you cannot go for this meal, it's the wrong meal, it's the wrong time, it's the wrong everything".*

So here I am. It's late already and the menu says there are five courses. *Five*! I shouldn't have five courses in a day! If I stay to the end there'll be no time for exercises or anything afterwards—at least they all know I'm teetotal so won't want me to go to the bar later, that should give me some time. I'm sure they won't mind if I go after the main course, and that will be mostly vegetables so that's not *too* bad. If I leave the meat but have the vegetables at least I've made the effort and that shouldn't take too much exercise to get it out of my system.

Right, starter—soup with bread roll. Don't like soup so that's easily evaded. Take the bread roll and put it aside for later. Yes, tell them I don't want to fill up before the rest of the meal. Very clever, just leave it to one side, maybe knock it under the table later. Maybe this won't be so difficult after all, looks like the vegetables are self service so that's good. Really is too late to be starting to eat, especially seeing as I need my four hour gap before I have my apple tonight. Can't be deflected from the routine. Have some vegetables and go, lovely job my son, you're doing so well.

This is not right. Look at all that meat, swimming in the oceans of gravy with big, huge stuffing balls full of calories. And what is that?! Sausage wrapped in bacon, or what looks like a huge slab of fat with slivers of bacon attached.

This is not right.

No vegetables thanks, I've got quite enough already.

So much noise, so much eating. How can they enjoy this so much? Maybe if I have a bit of chicken . . . No, this is all wrong, I need to get out right now, I'm not feeling well, this is too much pressure, I'm not ready for this, I need to go now.

John's Anorexia *"Go then, move, before they start asking questions. You were stupid to try this, why did you ever think you were ready. Once you are out of the hall, run to your room, get your coat and go for a* *walk. Get as far away from here, from all that food as possible. You are so pathetic, freaked out by one fat little sausage. There is no way you are ready to move on yet, no way. Look at what has just happened, one tiny step towards being fat and you couldn't handle it. You are nothing if you are not thin".*

"Nothing".

KIMMERIDGE COURT DIARY
WEEK 9

Into week 9 of my admission and things were really starting to become difficult. Throughout both admissions, rare have been the times when I have felt my weight and mental fortitude were progressing in unison, and the doubts about my ability to sustain my recovery in the "Real World" were by now really starting to emerge, just when my weight seemed to be accelerating to my BMI 20 target at an ever-increasing pace. I was starting to feel less contented at Kimmeridge Court and looking forward more to going home, which is always a positive sign, but the events of this week would do much to demonstrate how much work I still needed to do before I was ready to support myself.

All of which made the suggestion of staying to BMI 21 seem all the more surprising and, initially at least, preposterous.

Friday 12 February: Day 61

A day to show how tough this will be, but also why it's so vital that I do it. Things are tougher here in the "real world"; it's almost as if my brain gets switched from full on, nothing holding me back commitment to anxiety and doubts and Anorexia reasserting itself as my default setting. It all gets mixed in together—guilt, freedom, lack of support, memories—and it seems harder to see a way in which I can consider dipping my toe into exercise or calorie-counting without diving straight in. Then again, meeting Hannah, having a drink and going to the gig tonight (albeit alone) is what life can be about, not worrying about what I've eaten or whether I can allow myself to sit down. It is difficult to extricate myself from the past, but the past means nothing to me now—it's just a litany of missed chances, arguments and regrets. The rest of my life is scary, but scary is better than set in stone, especially when my predictable existence has been so detrimental to health, relationships and spirit.

Saturday 13 February: Day 62

Given how much my parents' stomachs rumbling put me on edge last week, seeming to block out all other noise as I sat there getting fatter, it seems ironic that when the same happens with me I almost get a feeling of euphoria. When my stomach rumbles it's like it's confirming my success, my willpower in resisting food even when I'm craving it. It gives me a justification to eat. I have forgotten what it feels like to be hungry or what it feels like to react to that hunger by eating outside my set mealtimes. Eating between meals has always been a no-go area and even with my more positive outlook at the moment, it remains something I would never consider.

I feel at a bit of a crossroads with my Anorexia. As ever, there are a hundred, a thousand reasons to change, and these get added to every day. Undoubtedly my life would be better without it, but there is still some appeal in the safety and conformity that the illness grants me. I'm still uneasy about inviting failure into my life, about letting go.

Sunday 14 February: Day 63

Bit of a turning point today, in that for the first time I didn't want to come back to the unit after my weekend at home. I am struggling to see what role I have here now, other than getting well and getting out. How quickly that will happen I don't know, and that is extremely frustrating. I'm so used to having complete control that to feel like this is all happening without any input from me is unnerving. More than ever I need to keep focused on what I have to do and ignore the "voice". This was a good weekend because I didn't have much time to fill, but how will I be on discharge? What happens when it's just me, and all my voice is saying is to give in? That will be when I know whether all this is worth the struggle.

Monday 15 February: Day 64

BMI: 18.9

I'm not going to lie and say I'm 100% happy with today's weight gain. Many of my old thoughts are still there—smaller and pushed further away—but there nonetheless and a 1kg gain in a few days raises all sorts of alarm bells about how much I'm going to have to eat and do when I hit maintenance. The bizarre thing about my situation is that I love food, and I have been concerned about how much I will have to cut out of my diet in order to maintain. My problem has rarely been with eating per se, just the supposed effect of eating. Anyway, at least I'm within sight of the finishing line now, and at least I have some evidence for the feelings of "fatness" that I do definitely feel more and more. I guess this must be my 18.9 body—it doesn't look horrific and I will start to accept it. I just have to maintain momentum.

As I approach "health" the fears that have plagued my life for the past fourteen years continue to slam themselves into my brain. I still feel horrible after a large meal, the sensation of being fatter, of my clothes feeling tighter still automatically sets alarm bells ringing. The truth is that I am setting a hell of a lot of trust in my ability to do this, to recognise the benefits of recovery and to use this knowledge to make changes and to ignore the voices until, others assure me, they will get quieter and quieter and eventually disappear. Unfortunately I have never proved that I have that ability and, whilst I believe things to be different this time, I can offer no guarantees. Nine weeks is not a massively long time to heal the problems with my parents, to "get over" my body image issues or to gain some self-esteem, but I'm getting so impatient about wanting to find out whether this is all a load of hot air. I like "John", but do I like him enough to keep "Anorexic John" from ever darkening my door again? I know that I cannot have a full life and be Anorexic. It's decision time.

PMA. PMA. PMA. PMA. PMA. PMA. Forward not back. PMA. PMA.

Tuesday 16 February: Day 65

I've definitely reached the turning point where I am counting down the days until I leave. As people move in and out and as I reach a healthy weight I feel more detached from the issues and worries that are part of everyday life here. I'm actually looking forward to going back to work, getting some more structure to my day again and starting the next phase of my recovery. I need to know whether everything I've done these past nine weeks, everything I have built up in terms of belief in myself and in what I've been told is going to be worth anything.

Important today that I could cope with not going out. I know it means nothing until maintenance (and even then it means little) but my major priorities were a) time off unit and b) having space to listen to my music, not getting out just for exercise. It didn't matter, and that's what I have to keep reminding myself. It doesn't matter, in the grand scheme of my life, it really doesn't matter. Also, Emily asking me to go shopping with her was great—she offered, and though I felt I shouldn't impose, it really meant something—sometimes it's the little things that matter the most. Hell, maybe someone does like me!

Wednesday 17 February: Day 66

If I'm honest I don't really feel any worse about myself and my body than I did nine and a half weeks ago. As time goes by it becomes more and more clear to me that this whole thing is not about how fat or thin I am, but how I feel about myself and how I have used my weight as a basis for my self-esteem. I feel so good about myself as a person here that I can sometimes disregard what is happening with my weight. In the real world, where I have nothing strong enough to counter the words in my head, I cling onto my weight as my one piece of evidence that I am strong, successful and different. I need to believe in myself more, in my qualities as a person, or I will keep coming back to Anorexia and my life will never move on.

Major alarm bells tonight when Laura (*staff member*) asked if I wanted to get something from downstairs. Suddenly my Anorexia kicked in, begging me to go straight away, right now before the moment to exercise had passed. I soon rationalised this feeling, and I have subsequently turned down a similar opportunity, but I haven't felt that urge for a long while. Thing is, moments like that, the sudden rush of excitement, the chance to prove to everyone how helpful, how fit, *how thin I am*, are really the closest I get to a high in my life. I have to find another high.

Thursday 18 February: Day 67

BMI: 19.3

More mixed feelings about my weight today. Having come to the point where I feel ready to leave, any step further forwards is positive, but the rate at the moment is concerning. I thought it was meant to get harder as you got heavier, but if anything my weight gain is accelerating. If I didn't like food so much it wouldn't be so much of a problem but, given the dangers involved in allowing exercise back into my life, it looks as if I may end up eating less than I did before I was admitted, which is kind of ironic! I feel no different now really to how I did last week, and it's quite reassuring to know that I've only got about two kilos left. I am beginning to worry, though, that my body is starting to race ahead of my brain again, and last night Anorexia gave me a stark warning that he ain't going away anywhere soon.

How do I replicate the ego boost in the "real world" where I'm being shouted at in work and not being told how well I'm doing simply by eating and sitting still? It's a question I've never been able to answer and I don't know if I have any better idea of how to answer it now. My past problems are like a huge elephant in the corner, overshadowing all the positive talk and the sense of belief. I know there will be times when it all seems too hard, when Anorexia seems to be the only solution to life's problems, and it is then that I will need to call in my support. I've managed to convince myself so much that recovery is inevitable, but getting there is going to be so lengthy and difficult I am going to have to summon up untapped levels of strength—to ignore the voice and the criticism—and to allow me to move on. How much of an ego boost will it be coming back here in a year's time, recovered and able to give something back? I can do it. I will do it.

I don't know whether to feel as high as a kite or really despondent. I certainly wasn't expecting an offer to stay to BMI 21, and it's sent my head spinning in a completely new direction. This is really where my belief in myself is going to be tested. If they're prepared to give me this opportunity it must mean i) they think it would benefit me ii) they are happy for me to be around and iii) they think I can handle it. Work is certainly an issue, as is any future career change, but really it all comes down to whether I believe in myself and my ability to cope in the outside world at a BMI of 21. It's not something I've ever given any consideration to. This admission was to get to BMI 20 and then go. In many ways BMI 21 is as scary to me now as BMI 15 was six months ago. I really will be putting my faith in myself and in what I am being told if I do this. I don't want to deprive anyone of a bed whilst I struggle versus an unbeatable foe, but I've got to decide whether it is unbeatable.

PMA.

Forward not back. Keep on going.

OUT OF THE FRYING PAN . . . .

I had absolutely no idea about what my time at Kimmeridge Court would involve, though my reluctant acceptance that I "may" put on weight was very swiftly countered by my Therapist who assured me that that would very definitely be happening! I hadn't shared a room for about 20 years so was quite relieved to find that, as the only male on the unit, I was put in single accommodation and given sole access to the best shower (sorry ladies). This relief was only matched by finding out that Art Therapy was no longer part of the programme, and when I was put on half portions for the first week, suddenly it didn't seem so bad!

The first couple of weeks were a bit strange, as I was probably eating less than I had been before I was admitted. Even more of a shock to the system, of course, was the complete restriction on exercise of any kind—rarely have I felt as if I would be letting so many people down just by standing up! It amazed me that I had cycled for miles the day before I was admitted and yet now I almost had to ask for permission to move. Anorexia had, of course, blinded me from the damage I had been doing to myself, even when, in the case of my osteoporosis, it was written down in black and white and writ large in the form of the tablets I had had to hand in on admission. I never considered disobeying the orders of the staff—I was "on board" at least to that extent—and the ball I took in with me was kicked only once a day in accordance with my good luck ritual (which clearly wasn't working!).

As per the first stages of the programme, I was not allowed outside of the building, which given my insatiable desire for "fresh air" was particularly hard to contemplate and cope with. I had some stuff to do from work and filled much of the rest of my time with jigsaws and board games, but the inability to exercise still left a yawning gap in my days. Deep down it was a massive relief to be given a break from my life, and such was the overwhelming sense of exhaustion that came over me in the first couple of weeks, part of me began to relish the fact that I had no choice but to sit down and rest. A tiny part of my soul had always wanted rid of Anorexia, whilst never believing that the risk of letting go offered enough of the control and the guarantees that were such an important part of my existence. If I had truly felt there was a life beyond Anorexia for me, I feel sure I would have tried harder to fight back.

The staff made it remarkably easy for me and I was constantly reassuring myself that the issue of guilt, which had done so much to undermine any previous attempts to fight back, was of no relevance here given that I had no choice in what I was being asked to do. Things got easier as my weight began to increase and I began to participate in therapy groups, which at least gave me back some of the structure that had been such a mainstay of my previous existence. Again I felt at no disadvantage being a male within these groups and found the chance to discuss my Anorexia in front of others who knew what it was like to feel as if eating was the very worst thing in the world was of great comfort.

My Anorexia, however, remained strong, and when I was allowed to begin to bring physical activity back into my day to day routine I made sure that each and every opportunity was taken, especially when I was given a list of gentle leg and arm exercises to do. I even attended every session of yoga and the dreaded "Stretch and Relax", simply because it avoided any more sitting down than was necessary. Towards the end of my admission I also joined the food management group, where we would make a meal for all of us in one of the two sessions, and then cook for ourselves in the other. I had no problems cooking for myself and enjoyed the opportunity of coming up with increasingly bizarre food combinations, but I felt very uneasy about cooking for other people and especially portioning it out in case someone felt I had given them too much. I certainly didn't contemplate taking any of the lessons I learned on portion sizes or getting a more balanced diet back with me to the "real world". As had been the case for years, I fixated on calories and I remained steadfast in my belief that I must not go over the 2000 daily calorie limit given for an average woman (I was small so clearly wouldn't need all an average man would be required to eat). I did make certain changes—full fat milk instead of watered-down skimmed and 450 calories instead of 250 for my main meal, but still everything had to be weighed and calculated and weighed again just to be sure.

My fellow "inmates" were, generally speaking, a supportive, inspirational bunch who seemed to put aside any misgivings they may have had about accepting a male into their world and made me feel welcome from the off. I tried to establish a niche for myself as the joke-telling, emotionally strong person on the unit and I think I bluffed it pretty well! Broadly speaking, the group divided into two, with those, including myself, who were "first-timers" and who had little concept of water-loading, diuretics and the whole panoply of eating disorder behaviours that some of the other group, many of whom had been serial "inmates", either continued to indulge in or spoke in great detail about. Finding myself among others who had a far deeper knowledge and experience of the illness troubled me at first, as I genuinely felt that they may perceive me as something of a fraud, especially as I evidently found certain aspects of the programme easier to conform to than other people. This was really the first time when my Anorexia was brought into close contact with that of other people, but because I felt Kimmeridge Court helped to suppress the negativity that usually engulfed my mind, it allowed me to attempt to pull others up with me, rather than be dragged down into the pit of behaviours and emotions that some were experiencing.

Life on the unit was superficially harmonious but there was a definite undercurrent of tension which, as a male, I could largely stay out of. Support times, which took place after every meal and which were supposed to offer a nourishing environment (forgive the expression) for those who were finding things particularly difficult, were especially fraught, often descending into group attacks on whoever's habits were supposedly upsetting everyone else at the time. At this time I was continuing to pace my eating so that I finished as near as possible to the 45 minute deadline we had before entering support, as I didn't feel comfortable sitting with nothing to do when others were still eating. I had maintained this behaviour since my admission so I was quite surprised to find it suddenly becoming an issue about seven weeks in, especially as those affected had given me no indication in private that there had been a problem. I was supported by others on the unit, but of course I should have done more to address this and the countless other behaviours that I still engaged in.

Truth is, although I was gaining weight and recognising the benefits accruing from this, I don't think I ever truly believed that I would completely recover, and sharing time and living space with women on, in some cases, their fifth or sixth admission, made it all seem even more impossible than before I was admitted. I knew I would never get "that bad" but still the thought of having no hang-ups over my weight and shape seemed so alien that to try a tackle each and every aspect of the illness appeared pointless. Best tackle the major one—my weight—and take it on from there later on.

Having established my role as the joker in the pack, my happy equilibrium was shattered by the admission of another male patient. I was taken from my single room with marvellous shower facilities to share a much smaller room and then one with the coldest en suite shower in the world when he was put on bed rest. I did little to disguise my hostility, which I recognise now stemmed largely from my fear that his arrival would displace me from my perch. Having avoided female contact for so long I was really enjoying being in that environment and had surprised myself at how well I had integrated. To be honest, I didn't feel like sharing that with anyone else.

My roommate found it really hard to follow the programme and his constant standing and loud music did little to endear him to anyone else, and I did little to disguise quite how irritated I was by his presence. Frankly, his background reflected mine so closely that it became extremely difficult to continue ignoring the seriousness of my own situation as I had thus far. He too had over-exercised in the pursuit of acceptance and popularity and his position right in the clutches of Anorexia represented a possible scenario that I found it uncomfortable to see for myself. Before being admitted I had existed quite happily in my own anorexic world and, whilst recognising that I was missing out on so much, I never thought that I was in any real danger. Kimmeridge Court shattered those illusions by showing me how dangerous Anorexia really was, how its impact can last not just one or two years but decades. If I'm honest, my roommate freaked me out. He would be discharged and readmitted before my twelve weeks were done, and as I became healthier I did find my stance towards him softening. I was given the opportunity to explain how his refusal to comply with the programme was affecting my own recovery, but I didn't feel comfortable putting his health at any more risk. However badly he was entrenched in his Anorexia, I knew that forcing him out would do little to improve his situation and, to be honest, I didn't want that on my conscience. Nevertheless, I was far from disappointed to regain my sole male status when he left.

I reached my target of BMI 20 and maintained for a short while before discharge. At the time I looked upon my agreeing to enter the eating disorders unit as the best decision I had ever taken but, in hindsight, I can see that my first admission was a huge missed opportunity. I had told my employers that I would be absent for three months and, whilst they were very accommodating about that and about a phased return to work, I did feel under a lot of pressure to leave Kimmeridge Court before I felt ready. I had achieved my physical goal of reaching a healthy weight, but I largely paid lip service to making the changes that would undermine my eating disorder.

Part of the reason that my Anorexia had developed and been sustained for so long was that it had fed into my desire, almost my need to be evidently the best at something I did. What started with schoolwork and football knowledge became far more damaging when I began to base my entire self-esteem on the fact that I was the thinnest, most strongly willed person at school, at University and then at work. There is no doubt that I drew huge self-confidence and pride from being able to say, without fear of contradiction, that I was the thinnest person I knew. Kimmeridge Court blew these truths out of the water, as I was suddenly surrounded by others who had taken the art of being thin and being self-disciplined to a level beyond anything I had "achieved". And, I began to realise, they had reached a point that I really did not want to get to, a mark that I really wasn't sure I had it in me to push on to. And, having reached that conclusion, I needed a new "Best" to present to the world. The failure of my first admission was routed in my inability to find a new goal to aim for.

I thought Kimmeridge Court was going to be a magic wand that would wash my Anorexia away and didn't appreciate the hard work I would have to continue to do in order to ensure that this was my one and only admission. I got caught up in the relentless positivity about how well I'd done and how strong I was being and just assumed that now I was a healthy weight my brain would sort itself out and I would be able to carry on where I left off with my exercise and eating. It doesn't matter how physically fit you are or even how positive you feel or how much of your willpower you retain. The possibility and fear remains, however tiny, that your weight could continue escalating and Anorexia doesn't just disappear into the ether. This is not something of huge concern in itself, but if, like me, you do nothing to undermine the fear of "fatness" that lies at the root of the eating disorder, you will never truly move on. I couldn't let Anorexia go because it remained my greatest defence against my ultimate fear.

My first admission definitely helped prepare me for my second, four years later, and without it I would have never have met my best friend and many others who have become very important people in my life, but I cannot escape the fact that if I had really committed myself then to battling the roots of my illness, that second admission may not have been necessary. What I thought I'd found was another stand-out achievement—I was the "Best Kimmeridge Patient Ever", one admission and everything sorted and wonderfully popular to boot. To preserve that status, all I had to do was to avoid going back.

Whatever happened, never go back.

KIMMERIDGE COURT DIARY
WEEK 10

A pivotal week in many different ways. My first long weekend at home meant cooking for myself five times as well as continuing the takeaway challenge with a kebab. My thoughts were dominated by the decision over whether to extend my admission until my BMI reached 21—beyond anything I had ever imagined myself capable—while at the same time being confronted with the re-emergence of old and unwelcome thoughts regarding my weight and appearance. In particular, would my weight spiral out of control once I had reached my target, whatever that I decided that would be, and did I honestly believe myself to be capable of carrying this through?

Friday 19 February: Day 68

I've had a day to sleep on it (*staying to BMI 21*) and I still don't know what to do. My gut instinct is definitely to stay on as I believe I can do it and that it would be good for me. At the moment it feels as if it would take a staff member telling me it was a bad idea for me to refuse the chance if offered. So why do I keep seeking reassurance? I don't feel like I want anyone to dismiss the idea, but maybe I'm still scared of failing, of pushing myself again only to find that the next time it is too far. Again it comes down to this: do I believe I can do it? If I truly believe, there can only be one option.

I do believe, but at the same time I'm really scared. I know if I mess up this time it's forever, and while I have plans in place and the backing of so many people, it still comes down to me versus my Anorexia, and the voice can still be heard loud and clear. I wish I could just let go, realise how crap my life has been and use that as motivation, but that's never been enough and never will be. Unless I believe, I will never have the power to get through the down times. Clearly there are people who believe in me, but do I? This feels like it could be the biggest week of my life.

Saturday 20 February: Day 69

I always assumed that as I got nearer a healthier weight this would get easier, but it seems as if the opposite is true. The voice is getting stronger and more frequent. I'm not sure I would have done the Kebab Challenge if it wasn't for Abbie's support, but I suppose I have to use all tools available. In some ways I feel in control but in others my life seems a total screw-up. How will I deal with work? What the hell is happening with my hormones at the minute? I've got a really important decision to make about BMI 21, and all I can think about is a girl that I like. Bloody hell!

You're such an inspiration John. Thank you so much for meeting me, you gave me just the boost I needed. We can both do this, it really is different this time.

Margot

Sunday 21 February: Day 70

It's days like today that will decide how and to what extent I recover. After the "Pizza Incident" (*where I felt I'd over eaten*), every thought ran through my mind—*walk further, check yourself, weigh yourself, eat less, check the calories*—and it has been really hard to resist this (so far). At the moment I can take that step back and look at the evidence: I'm still putting on weight (especially if I continue to BMI 21); I'M NOT FAT; one meal does not obesity cause. Whether I can still do this months down the line is going to be the key to whether this really is different or whether it's all a load of hot air.

A really tough day, with lots of reminders of how it used to be, probably the toughest this admission. I've really been tested, have failed at times and felt really uneasy about my new body shape. However, I can still see that I have thin parts of my body, I can still rationalise my weight gain, and the possibility of reaching BMI 21 has actually eased the pressure a bit. It's not been a good day, but it has ended well and it's friends like Hannah who make it worthwhile. It's precisely because I don't want days like this that I have to keep going. It is, and I am, worth it.

Monday 22 February: Day 71

I seem to bounce from one extreme to the other at the moment. Most of the time I'm on cloud nine and absolutely nothing seems impossible. It is easy to reflect on my illness, to pinpoint the downsides and map out exactly what it has done to ruin my life. And yet there remain under the surface all the doubts and the self-criticisms that have ruled over me for so long. At the moment I can largely dismiss them, but the fear is still there that one, three, six months down the line the impact of all the good work and the good words will be subsumed by the day-to-day reality of living alone with my brain. I can come up with a whole host of strategies to counter this, but it will come down to the same thing as last time—when it comes to the crunch, will I make the right choice, or the easy one?

Tuesday 23 February: Day 72

BMI: 19.5

Again mixed feelings about weight. I'm glad it hasn't gone down and that momentum is still forward, but after the weekend I kind of wanted more reward for my effort. Now I've decided to go for BMI 21, I almost can't wait to get there and test myself, but I have to keep telling myself that this is not a race. It's almost as if I have again swapped the "competition" of being slim for one of being the best at Kimmeridge Court, which means I must betray no hint of weakness and have to keep putting on weight relentlessly else I might not be seen to be totally "on message". Am I kidding myself? I hope not, and I don't believe I am, but I've got a while to go yet. BMI 21 is such an abstract concept that I have no idea how it will be, but then BMI 19.5 seemed a world away two months ago. Now is not the time to make life decisions.

Thursday 25 February: Day 74

BMI: 19.5

I do feel as if I have come far on this admission, and I hope and believe that the changes I am making will pay off in the end. Even so, the thought of doing this for a whole year, of staying in this mindset and maintaining the pressure for all that time seems extremely daunting and unrealistic. The only way I can conceive of it is by thinking day-to-day, of going to bed every night with one more strike on the total, of having got through one more day without giving in to Anorexia. I am now entering completely unknown territory, and I have no idea how I am going to feel or how I will react. I have to keep it all at the forefront of my mind—the plus points, the friends, the good words—and hope and hope and hope it's enough to override the fear and the doubts and the thoughts that spring instantly to mind as soon as I see myself in the mirror or notice a bit more weight in different areas. At the same time this seems both the easiest and most difficult thing in the world. I've never been "normal", so I have no idea how to do a job, how to be sociable, how to ask a girl out. This is all stuff I am having to learn at the same time as fighting the biggest enemy I have ever faced, one which I haven't yet come close to defeating.

I've just sat through probably the best therapy group I've ever had the pleasure to be part of. Some of the stories, the discussions were really inspiring and the strength of character and human spirit were brilliant. I made naff all contribution, partly because anything I said would have sounded really lame and partly because I'm not sure how well I can presently relate to the issues being aired. I've said about my family and how much I believe in myself and how the only way to heal the rifts is to prove myself to them a thousand times, I'm almost sick of hearing myself say it. Fact is, I'm a very lucky person who has a fantastic chance to live a fantastic life. Am I really going to throw that away?

ANOREXIA'S CALL

You can listen to all the talk of fighting me and leaving me behind, you may even pretend to agree and play along, but you know you will never be rid of me. You're not strong enough, you've always been too weak to fight back, that's why they always picked on you, but then what did you expect? You wore glasses, you cried, you were fat and you always went running back to mummy. Until I came along you were hopeless. Didn't it all stop when you lost weight, all the name calling, all the nastiness? That's what I did for you, and you know all you have to do for me is to keep going, to let nothing and no-one come between us.

Just stick to the rules. Never risk any occasion with food, think of an excuse—parents staying, feeling ill, already eaten—you'll think of something. Why would you want to spend time with them, eating, when you could be with me, exercising? If you started to walk while you ate, the calories would barely register. That thing we have going with the washing up, where you walk while drying, let's go faster, let's put the washing basket further from the line and take each individual item of shopping upstairs one by one. You're not doing *enough*, you can go *further*, you have to push *harder*. Standing is good, uses more energy than sitting down. No more than six hours sleep, think of all that energy burning potential you lose while lying in bed.

How good does it feel to be the one with willpower, the one being healthy and doing their week's exercise every day, while everyone else is out there being obese and going from bed to car to office to car to sofa to bed? Doesn't it excite you to be the one that cycles to work, who always takes the stairs and never, ever accepts a sweet? It's almost like you stand taller than everyone, above all the others who are fatter than you are. They may have more money, more friends, more stuff, but they will never be as thin as you.

And stop whining about never getting a moment's peace. You know that all you have to do to keep me quiet is to do exactly as I say, that's all I want from you. Go on, just put those extra couple of crisps in the bin like you thought about, and I promise to leave you alone. It's only because you do stupid things that I hang around all the time. Go on, put them in, right to the bottom past all the regurgitated bread from earlier, right down so they'll be crushed and you won't be tempted to fish them out later like the little glutton you are. There, that wasn't too difficult was it? And now, I'll disappear, just like I promised, see ya!

BOO!

Ha, you fell for it didn't you? You *actually* thought you could get rid of me just like that?! You're more gullible than I thought! Why would I leave you for a second, just so you could go off and be the fat person that you really are? No chance, mate, I'm here for keeps. And why would you want rid of me anyway? I am you. I'm the best friend you'll ever have—I protect you, keep you from embarrassing yourself or becoming fat or showing everyone how weak you really are. You know no-one else really likes you, not if you're fat, not if you're you.

Now, about that walk . . . .

KIMMERIDGE COURT DIARY
WEEK 11

Another week of keeping on keeping on, with familiar fears about my weight and my life outside Kimmeridge Court continuing to return with their old potency. Still, though, I managed to fight back, undoubtedly helped by the improved mental capacity afforded me by my now healthy weight, as well as constant reminders from good friends of exactly what it is that I am fighting for. Oh yeah, and I reached my original target weight. Which was nice.

Friday 26 February: Day 75

It was good to see you—you cheered my day up heaps. I will always be here through the good and the bad.

Hannah

Saturday 27 February: Day 76

Strange old day, where my concerns re: Anorexia seemed minimal and yet remain lurking in the background, ready to spring forward whenever I look in the mirror or eat "a lot". I wish I could say that everything was hunky dory, but I don't like the way I look, I still get a buzz from exercise or simply not sitting down. Eleven weeks and counting and recovery remains both the easiest and the hardest thing. I am still scared of putting on weight and everything spiralling out of control. I say I just want a "normal" life, but will I really settle for that, or will I always be disappointed in myself? Unless I do learn to appreciate my qualities and what I have achieved, I don't think recovery is realistic. I have the evidence that I am liked—I have to use it.

Sunday 28 February: Day 77

As I get nearer "recovery", I am becoming increasingly aware of the moments and circumstances in which I am most vulnerable to the old voices. Having a bath, in particular, where I have a great deal of contact with my naked body, is currently quite a distressing experience. Being ill or full or having indigestion brings about a heightened anxiety which makes it difficult to think clearly about my Anorexia. Occasional poor decisions e.g. stairs rather than escalator, still produce an undeniable frisson of excitement. My body is undoubtedly showing signs of "health" and I am feeling fat in places where I can't remember experiencing it before. Standing up I'm ok and can recognise that most of it is muscle. Day by day, with other things to distract me or when I'm covered in clothes I don't notice it, nor when I'm happy and/or singing. I honestly don't view myself as "fat" and I know I will adjust to it if I give it time, but it is proving harder to accept my body than I had anticipated it would.

Monday 1 March: Day 78

Since I've come to recognise a change in my motivation and belief about my recovery, I've been searching for a cause or a reason for this change. Just saying I changed my mind is too simplistic and glib an answer and insults the battle that I and other sufferers have faced and continue to face. I still can't fully explain it, but I think once I overcame the shame of returning to Kimmeridge Court, once I swallowed my pride over going back, other "impossible" decisions seemed to become possible. Once I recognised the huge effort that I was putting into my Anorexia, I could begin to question my motivation and whether I could apply the same effort to my recovery—because that is what it will take to beat this. Once I was given a break from my Anorexia I had time to really think and reflect and concede that I have been humiliated enough and that what is done is done. The past has been crap but the future might not be.

Tuesday 2 March: Day 79

BMI: 19.8

Another weekend, another kg, but at least it means there is a legitimate reason behind the feelings I'm having. I'm almost at BMI 20 now, with

3½ kg to go to BMI 21. I am about to enter uncharted territory and it's getting scary. My fear now is less about everything spiralling out of control and I know that once I become more active I will plateau out, but I have definite concerns about what I will look and feel like in three or four weeks' time. I have coped ok so far, but will I cope with this, can I really resist the paranoia, the belief that everyone is looking at me?

I can point to a hundred things I have done differently on this admission, positive moves I've made and risks that I've taken that I have never before contemplated, but still all I can base my predictions on is a history of failure. Looking at it like that it's almost as if I'm operating on blind faith, but something is different, something within me which I can't really put into words. At the moment I can usually block out the voice, but that just makes the moments it returns even more threatening.

Wednesday 3 March: Day 80

Not feeling so great today. I am tired, but I think I just feel more conscious of my physical "improvement". Fact is that some of the parts of my body of which I was most proud—jaw line, ribs—are being fleshed out and it's difficult not to focus on this rather that the more positive aspects. I can see in the mirror that I look "normal"—and that is good—but some days recovery just seems so hard versus Anorexia which is easy and has been my life for so long. Recent events should make me reflect on how precious life is, but Anorexia does not allow for such blue sky thinking. Life is short and Anorexia screams at you that that life has to be thin. It amplifies all the health warnings about obesity and alcohol and hides those about the dangers of being underweight. I don't feel like I want to do the wrong thing, just not so enthusiastic about doing the right thing instead.

Talk of a balanced lifestyle (*in Health Awareness Group*) is always a good reminder, but as with so many of the benefits of a healthy life, it's nothing we don't already know. I want all the elements in my life, and I expect my life in recovery to include them, but when recovery does not appear to be an option, when you don't believe it can ever happen, you accept whatever life gives you and try to live within the boundaries Anorexia sets for you.

PMA. Forward not back. I WILL BEAT THIS.

Thursday 4 March: Day 81

BMI: 20

A big day. I've reached my original target of BMI 20, so I should now be counting down the days until my discharge. Instead I've got another 3½ kg to go, and I'm already uneasy about how I look. Because I am now entering unchartered territory, all my old fears about how much difference each extra 100g is going to make to my appearance are coming back. I don't want to over-dramatise this, I will get to BMI 21, but will I like what I see when I get there, especially as I am having doubts already? All logic tells me that I won't explode, that all those blokes down the pub (*night before, pub quiz*) looked perfectly fit. I know that the difference between 42 kg and 56 kg has not been massive, so why should 56 kg to 60 kg be any worse? Again and again, this comes down to my belief in myself and my determination to beat this once and for all. If I want to keep a tiny bit of my Anorexia in my life, if I want to preserve some of the safety and security it gives me, I will ask to go now. That's exactly what I did last time, and look where it got me. Truth is, there is no good reason to keep Anorexia and so, so many brilliant, fantastic ones to let it go that really there's no question. I will beat this.

Been thinking a lot about how much my self-esteem is connected to my body image. My Anorexia definitely does not like what it sees in the mirror, but I can see the improvement when I am wearing clothes. I look ok, if anything still a bit thin in the arms and legs. This weekend at home may be tough, my Anorexia may be stronger than ever, but this is why I need to spend time with friends like Hannah and Abbie, who make me happy just by agreeing to spend time with me. It's times like those that anything seems possible, at others almost impossible. All I can do is to keep going and trust in everyone at Kimmeridge Court. They haven't let me down yet. 20% fear, 80% EXCITEMENT. Hold onto that.

NEW BEGINNINGS

As I approached the end of my admission and my scheduled return to work, I started to realise that I didn't want to go back, indeed that I hadn't been enjoying my job for a very long time. Mistakes had led to criticisms which had undermined my already fragile self-esteem, and I greeted each new day with an ever-increasing sense of dread at what I would do wrong next. Everyone at work had been so supportive of me during my time in hospital and were so happy to see me healthy and back in the office, but the place held too many memories of how I'd been and how my illness had dragged down my performance. Truth was my relationship with my manager would never have recovered given the huge record of mistakes and odd behaviours I had displayed in the previous two and a half years. If my "recovery" was to mean anything then I had to have a new start, in a job where I could utilise the personal qualities I had unearthed whilst in Kimmeridge Court and in which I actually cared about what I was doing. My three month notice period was like purgatory and it was only the thought of leaving and the nights out I was having with my new friends from Kimmeridge that kept me sane. That and my absolute conviction that I was beating my Anorexia.

My choice of new career was made on the basis of the care and support shown to me from the staff at Kimmeridge. As I was so clearly winning my battle with the illness, I felt as if I would be able to give something back and to help others experiencing the same mental tortures as I had. I also appreciated that my self-esteem still needed bolstering, and I saw nursing as an excellent career from which to enhance my own good feelings about myself. I knew that I would be unable to undertake a mental health nursing course until I had proved my recovery was for real, so set about getting some experience by becoming a healthcare assistant at the local general hospital. I also started a home study course on Eating Disorders, ostensibly to reintroduce myself to academic study. Of course I didn't really have to do much research to produce work that I was told was a "pleasure to mark", but I never completed the course due in the main part to the amount of sitting down it would require to finish.

My hours at the hospital were irregular and, because the long stretches of inactivity on the wards left lots of time for unhelpful thoughts to re-emerge, I got a second job, shelf-stacking in the evenings at a large store. My weight had stayed relatively stable during my three month notice period at the County FA, as I was sat down for much of the day and socialising rather than exercising after work. It did not take long for my momentum to lapse as I embraced my new, more energetic routine.

I settled into a pattern of working in the hospital from 8 until 1, on my feet constantly with my break affording me the opportunity to go outside for some "fresh air". I would then cycle home, grab something to eat before a quick stroll and then walking to my second job where I spent the next four hours until 9 o'clock fetching and carrying stock. This was done in a very anorexic way, with my stock placed a long way from the shelf and no more than four items at a time taken from the box. I managed to bluff my way past my supervisor's queries about my behaviour and even invented a fear of confined spaces to explain my reluctance to use the lift!

There were fewer opportunities to indulge my Anorexia at the hospital, though I did everything I could to avoid sitting down for a second and there were undoubtedly occasions in which patient safety came a very distant second to the demands of the illness. My inability to address my behaviours in terms of eating—4hours between each meal, eating in a very slow, measured manner—meant I was always rushing to get to and from work, especially when I felt I needed to do some more exercise if I hadn't done "enough" during the day. My new work pattern also had the effect of decimating my still embryonic social life, and I found less and less time for other people in amongst my new, "healthier", routine.

None of this concerned me, of course, convinced as I was that my recovery was complete and permanent. Anorexic thoughts continued to direct my day and my behaviour, but I had never seriously believed that they would disappear altogether and I still felt safe indulging my illness within certain parameters. I had reached a point in my fight against Anorexia beyond which I had no intention of going and saw no need to push things any further. Life wasn't perfect but at least it felt like a life and not just an existence, and I would always have my "success" at Kimmeridge as proof of my worth. My recovery, at least, would be perfect.

My laissez-faire attitude did not convince everybody, however, and my therapist soon expressed her concerns about the path I was taking. In truth

I had quickly adopted a new, even more destructive routine which allowed little room for other people or interests beyond work and exercise. I did start a voluntary job with a homeless charity on Saturdays as part of my plan to "put myself out there", but as my working week began to reach 45 hours something had to give. I had become so convinced of victory over my Anorexia I ignored all the signs of its presence, even when my weight began to fall back. The loss was almost imperceptible and so I happily disregarded my therapist's concerns, assuring her that I would slow down and put the weight on but once again finding myself utterly incapable of doing so. I was still a healthy weight and I knew that I would never get "that bad" again, but I was already restricting and my days were back in a pattern of exercising, eating and work. Nothing, though, could penetrate the recovery bubble I was living in. I knew I would be ok.

My weight loss was gradual enough for me to bluff my way through my now monthly therapy sessions and, a year after my discharge from the inpatient unit, both my therapist and I concluded that I was no longer getting anything constructive from my meetings with her. My appointments had settled into a pattern of being weighed, discussing why I thought my weight had dropped, my therapist expressing her fears that my Anorexia was taking over again and me assuring her that I would change something to help put the weight on. My therapist agreed to my request to discharge me from the outpatient service, though I would learn later that she had little faith in my ability to stay away forever. I however, remained convinced that I had found the magic formula and felt that, as I was a healthy weight, I could now do as much exercise as I wanted. I was aware that Anorexia continued to provide the structure to my days but I genuinely believed that if I indulged it enough so that I didn't feel the guilt then I would be able to live my life alongside it. Truth was that Anorexia's presence was now even more potentially destructive because I possessed an arrogance engendered by the way I had fought against it whilst at Kimmeridge Court. Away from there, I had neither the skills nor the fortitude to keep on fighting.

KIMMERIDGE COURT DIARY
WEEK 12

Another week of what was becoming a familiar pattern of contrasting emotions. To some degree I continued to be carried along on a wave of positivity—both mine and other peoples—and each extra step taken and each kind word, or in this case gift received, only added to my conviction that I must keep going. Even so, it would not take much to send me in completely the opposite direction, and fears about my appearance, my place within the group and my return to "normality" were very close to the surface, just waiting for weigh day for their chance to catapult forward once more.

Friday 5 March: Day 82

Although in some ways it is getting more difficult to do this, if I take a step back from the Anorexia, it is harder to see what it is that I get out of it. Yes, it does protect me from risks and from putting myself out there, but I am going to have to live at some point. If I work hard, *really* hard this year then I can have a life; if I start to slip now because I'm convinced I'm getting love handles then what's the point? Australia? Fantastic, but I've still got to face life at the end of it. Treat this year as one long new start. Use it right and you can do it.

Interesting group today describing how we are all driving a bus through life, upon which Anorexia is a passenger who spends the whole time distracting us and urging us to take a false turn and follow the path it wants us to take. If I'm honest, I've been a passenger on Anorexia's bus for the last fourteen years and in some ways it feels as if I've wrested control with no idea how to drive the bus or which destination it is that I'm heading to. At the moment the shiny, happy music on the bus is generally blocking the passenger out, but when I hit a hazard, he shoots forward again.

Came up with a really naff metaphor today: my life at the moment is a can of beans. There is some great end destination to which I am heading, and to get there I am building a pyramid out of cans of beans. Each positive decision I make, each bit of advice or knowledge or praise that I receive adds another can to the pyramid. The pyramid is getting nearer and nearer the destination but as this happens, the danger of a catastrophic collapse is also greater, and every wrong decision takes away a can of beans, which can bring the whole thing crashing down.

There is no doubt that things are harder at home. Recovery seems less inevitable, there is more room for doubt. Loads of encouragement and kind words today, and that is all a boost, but I don't know yet if it's enough. I'm not fat, and the only time I'm worried is naked in front of the mirror. Why do I put myself through it *(looking in the mirror)*? My logic is that the more I get used to seeing myself as I am, the more comfortable I will be. I know the risks and I believe I can deal with them, but that doesn't make them any less dangerous or omnipresent. I've never been able to fight them back before.

Saturday 6 March: Day 83

A day of small but significant successes, from watching a film to having a bit extra to breaking the four hour rule, TWICE! It seems such a ridiculous rule to live my life by, but caught up in my Anorexia it is just so vitally important that I eat nothing until four hours after my last mouthful. All the other challenges I have taken on in this admission could be "justified" as helping me to put on weight, but this has nothing to do with reaching BMI 21. This was all about letting go of the control that has been exerted over my life, and the fact that I did it so that I could go out with my best friend makes it doubly significant. Quite exciting actually!

The sight of myself is no less shocking or distressing as time, and weight, goes on, but is it as distressing as I had feared? If I take the time to actually *look* at my body, I can see the good bits. As always, it is the fact that I am comparing me with me, not other people, which makes my physical improvement so difficult. Being told I look better is still a mixed blessing, but being told I look handsome is all good! My weight has been my safety blanket for so long that to let go is really frightening/exciting. Right now I feel ready to take that risk. I just hope this feeling can last.

Sunday 7 March: Day 84

It is taking a long time to get used to my body. Sometimes I look at my chest, from certain angles, and it looks all right; at others, it just looks fat and my fears about what it will be like 3 kg down the line come screaming back. If I was a normal, healthy bloke I would be able to do something to build up my muscle, maybe use some weights or sit-ups, but I honestly don't believe I can even tempt myself with old behaviours coming back. I know I've been getting all excited about what life without Anorexia might hold, but can exercise really be part of it? I have tried at various times to incorporate exercise as part of a healthy lifestyle, but it doesn't take long to become a question of targets and incessant, non-stop pressing. Will my recovery be complete without exercise? No, not really, but can I hope to recover with it in my life?

Good day, strange day. Some thoughts of old times, especially when doing the ironing, but no reaction and I did what I had to do. There is no doubt that my anxiety levels are increasing as I get nearer discharge, though whether this is because of my weight or my job I'm not sure. I am becoming used to my new shape, but I struggle to believe that it could be deemed attractive. I just seem so out of proportion at times.

Monday 8 March: Day 85

There it is! Definitive proof that someone does like you. A completely no obligation gift that was neither asked for nor expected, from someone that knows nothing about anorexic John, about all the rubbish of the last fourteen years. If I cock this up I want bloody shooting. I have to keep that letter for ever, because there will be times when I do doubt myself and when being thin again seems to be the root to happiness. It's at times like those that I need to remember moments like this, when someone praises me for something more, something better than what I look like.

My feelings about my weight, and more particularly my body shape, are swinging wildly at the moment. Most of the time it is not on my mind—in itself something of a revolution—and if a take a cold, hard look, especially without my head in shot, my abdomen does not look too bad. Sat down looking at myself in the mirror now I actually look like a man, and I don't think I've ever thought that before. But then, suddenly, I'll touch myself somewhere where there wasn't flesh before or catch a glimpse from another angle and all the old fears will come roaring back. I'm constantly reminded of quite how much faith I'm placing in my ability to get used to my new body, and there is a very real danger that months down the line, when the good vibes of Kimmeridge Court are long behind me, that I won't be able to summon up the strength to keep fighting. This is why I have to keep fighting. This is why I have to build up my resources now, keep the letter and remember all the really, really good things, because life will shit on me at some point. I've never been able to cope before—will it be different now?

Tuesday 9 March: Day 86

BMI: 20.5

Another huge weight gain which again gives rise to contrasting emotions. On the one hand I'm happy that I have a reason for feeling bigger and now with less than 2 kg to go the end is almost in sight. Once I become more active and go back to one cooked meal a day I'm sure things will balance themselves out. On the other hand, 1.3 KG IN FIVE DAYS! FUCK! I'm not eating much more than I used to, and yet my weight is, if anything, accelerating. I thought it was meant to get harder as I went along but it's almost the opposite. Does this mean I will have to return to my old activity levels if I want to eat what I used to? Can I even begin to consider risking that? Already I'm feeling uneasy about parts of my body, seeing what could do with a bit of firming up, and I really don't know if I can live on this tightrope for the foreseeable future.

Keep going, it can be done, YOU CAN DO IT.

Wednesday 10 March: Day 87

As I get nearer my target, the doubts and voices are starting to sneak in. Why did I not go for the biggest potato? Am I really going to hit the wall at the last? I'm so close now to the possibility of a life that I can almost smell it. All (ALL!) I have to do is to keep going as I have done, keep making the right decisions and IT WILL GET EASIER. I have to believe that if all this is not going to be in vain.

Thursday 11 March: Day 88

BMI: 20.7

I haven't really reflected on my role within my family too much, and certainly not linked it to my Anorexia. When I think about it, maybe it has suited me to fit into the "baby role", as this has allowed me not to take risks and to stay as a sixteen year old. By clinging to my mother's apron strings I've been able to live a half life, where I never totally feel as if I've left home. This is another reason why recovery is so important. If I'm going to be the man I can be, the man I should be, then Anorexia cannot be part of my life. It is so, so difficult to even conceive of the effort I am going to have to put in to beat this, how huge a shift in perspective it will take, but I can do it. I will do it.

ANOREXIA'S GIFT TO ME

Many accounts of Anorexia speak of black holes, of deep depressions and an acceptance of punishment for the sufferer's self—perceived worthlessness. Personally, I have never regarded my Anorexia as a deserved consequence of my own evil deeds. I simply felt that there was a certain amount of food that I could allow myself which would not lead me to put on weight. In order to justify that intake of food, and to build up my fitness, there was a certain level of exercise which had to be done every day, without fail, regardless of weather or lack of time. If for some reason e.g. travelling home on the train, I knew I would not be able to do as much exercise as usual, I would reduce my intake accordingly. By doing this I thought I could keep my Anorexia quiet, whilst remaining keenly aware of its presence, and this allowed me to spend what little spare time I had enjoying my existence, such as it was. So I did watch TV, I did listen to music and to the radio and I would sometimes even find time for my friends, all the time convincing myself that, while my Anorexia could never be beaten, I was making the best of it anyway. I had given up hope on relationships, a decent career, real friendships and family, effectively on life itself, but hey, I could still go for a walk every day.

Somewhere along the line I lost the capacity to enjoy life. I could have an amazing day, maybe seeing Everton win or getting a new job, but I always knew that any short-term shot of euphoria would eventually seep away to be replaced by *stand-up, run, exercise, starve*. It's very difficult to live in the moment when you can always see the massive BUT ahead in the road, always waiting to highlight your flaws and questioning your right to happiness. How many of these thoughts were Anorexia talking and how much of it stemmed from my lack of self-esteem I cannot answer; indeed the two issues have become so intertwined over the years that they are virtually indistinguishable. I disliked myself so I exercised to gain acceptance; I caused other people pain through my Anorexia, so clearly I was selfish and cruel.

What Anorexia does is grind down your hope, your ambition, your faith in yourself. I have stressed that I never wanted Anorexia nor consciously engineered its entry into my life, and for many years it was only this knowledge that kept me going. I knew Anorexia was ruining my life and those of people who cared for me, but I had no idea how to go about tackling it or, to be honest, any particular inclination to try until I felt "ready". I've lost count of the number of times I went to sleep with my head full of resolve to start fighting back in the morning, only to see it vanish very quickly when faced with the prospect of one more flake of cereal added to the bowl.

I had no faith in my own ability to fight this alone nor, for most of the last fifteen years, have I had any real support, and all I have been able to hang onto is the hope, the possibility that one day I would wake up and everything would have changed and I would feel ready to move on. I waited and waited for that day, reassuring everyone that I was actually doing really well and I was really happy, thank you for asking, but eventually I had to admit that the day would never come. And so I had to refocus my life: there would be no relationships, no huge salaries, no London Marathons or games of football; just Anorexia and me, doing a job I hated because it kept me on my feet all day and was the only thing I could do to stop the voices in my head, even for a second. All the self-esteem and self-love I had built up in my first Kimmeridge Court admission had been bulldozed away, my family and friends relegated to second place.

One thing I'm sure of, even if I do completely recover, is that I will never recapture the outlook on life that I had pre-diagnosis. Amongst the bullying and the concerns I had about how others perceived me, there remained moments of fun and happiness. Going to the football with Dad, having a laughing fit watching *Blackadder*, singing along to Oasis—certain memories come back when I get some reminder of the 90s, but there were none of these moments once Anorexia took hold. The constant, never-ending focus on the next meal, the next walk, the next potential obstacle to Anorexia's master plan gave me no time for enjoying any part of life that wasn't directed by the illness. In the past year I've started singing again (very badly). Football seems to matter again, in the moment if not at the expense of everything else. And I have laughed. Life is better now than it has been for as long as I can remember, but I don't think I will ever recapture the sense of invulnerability and hope that I once had. The 'John' of fourteen years ago has gone forever.

That is what Anorexia gave to me.

KIMMERIDGE COURT DIARY
WEEK 13

So close! Just when I thought I was on the brink of target time (and confidently told everyone of this), life had one more card up its sleeve to stop me from being too happy. So my stay at Kimmeridge would be extended for another week, and whilst I hunkered down for a bit longer, the friends I had come to feel very close to were starting to leave. I always found these occasions difficult: on the one hand you feel delighted that they are ready to leave, that they have the strength to keep on fighting in the "real world", but you know how much you will miss them and how much emptier your life will be without them there every day, which considering I didn't know them two months ago is quite something! More worries, more swearing, more great friends and compliments, more faith in my ability to fight this (despite locking myself out of my house. Doh!).

Friday 12 March: Day 89

There is a real mix of feelings going on now. On the one hand, the closer I get to BMI 21, to discharge, to work, to the real world, the more frightening this all seems and the harder it is becoming to make the right decisions. I feel as if I have to prove how "recovered" I am, to pick up life from where I left off and to almost ignore this has happened. On the other I'm so scared of going back, of what I will have to do to be happy and to live my life. In general, I can see my emotions for what they are, but there is no doubting the thrill I feel when there is a chance to eat less or exercise more.

All this, and yet every day continues to bring evidence that people like me now and the person I am now. Perhaps I have used my face as a defence mechanism, knowing that people would be struck/appalled by my features and not wish to probe any further and test the things I really cared about but dare not put up for scrutiny. How can I seriously believe that the people that matter, the ones I really care about, liked Anorexic John more than "John", whatever "John" represents? It's all out there for me, the chance to have a chance, and all I have to do is keep on keeping on, making the right decisions and this will be beaten. I can do it, I will do it, if not for me then for everyone who believes in me, loves me, has told me they've missed me or that I'm looking better. Of course it's hard, but IT IS NOT IMPOSSIBLE.

Saturday 13 March: Day 90

One of those days where everything seems possible. It's amazing how surrounding yourself with positive people puts you in such a good mood. So many good things said today, but the one with most resonance was Hannah saying she looked forward to seeing me now. Even I prefer me without Anorexia and I have no desire to go back there. I just wish I could be happier with how I look. As I keep telling myself, in time I will get used to it and I will learn to see that I'm not fat, which I'm not. It still doesn't beat back the thoughts when I catch myself in the mirror—*you're fat, disgusting, you've lost control, you will be a blimp.* I have no answers on how to break this other than to keep on keeping on, listening to what I am being told and try to accept praise when it comes. Everything I've ever wanted is there on a plate, but I'm the only one who can take it. Just do it.

> *U do make me blooming laugh . . . . defo good to have your support cause if I'm completely honest u help me get through the days . . . . think I should call you the legendary puzzle man!*
>
> *Abbie*

Sunday 14 March: Day 91

Another good, instructive day, in which I again passed challenges, changed plans and enjoyed myself. Meeting Hannah is always brilliant and a bit of retail therapy is always good. I definitely feel more confident about how I look and about putting myself out there. What she said yesterday is still resonating and if I could just bottle what I'm feeling right now then everything would be fine.

Locking myself out of my house today at least shows me that everything will not be sweetness and light just because I'm "recovered". I will still forget things, still make stupid, STUPID mistakes but that's life and if I keep this up that is what I will have—life.

Tuesday 16 March: Day 93

BMI: 20.9

Almost there! Two days to put on at least 0.3 kg and then it's countdown to discharge. So many thoughts going through my head it's difficult to know how to look upon this. Excitement, definitely, about going home, about the possibilities ahead of me, about giving things and getting praise. Sadness too, I've made some really good friends here and not to see them every day is always a wrench. Fear, though, is still very much there and getting bigger. I've made all sorts of plans but they all ultimately depend on me and how I decide to act. Will I really make the right choices six months down the line? Once I become more active will I be able to suppress the urge to go further, go harder, keep pushing the boundaries of my physical capabilities? Can I really, honestly, see myself not exercising for a whole day or having a snack out? No matter how optimistic I feel about things, the memories of my first admission keep slamming back into my mind. So far I have a 100 per cent failure rate, and while my belief is definitely greater, is it that much different to how I felt just before my first discharge? I had the same dreams, expectations, good words, but none of it was enough to stop Anorexia from screwing my life up once again. There is also a very real fear that this won't stop at BMI 21, that my body will want to keep going until it reaches its "natural weight", whatever astronomical figure that may be. I'm still learning to live with my body in its new, enlarged state and while some parts do get more familiar, others still shock me and instantly bring Anorexia's booming voice back into play.

Wednesday 17 March: Day 94

I have no idea about whether my "recovery" is all a sham or whether it really is for real. What I do know is that being with Hannah makes me feel good, but being healthier when I see her makes me feel ten feet tall. Not feeling like I have to rush off or go for a walk because we haven't been "far enough" and not worrying about cancelling things because she wants to see me. She WANTS to see ME, sod anything else.

Thursday 18 March: Day 95

BMI: 20.8

FUCK. Probably the worst day of this admission, where occasionally I have felt as if I have taken on too much and where the thought of work and the real world has at times seemed too horrific to contemplate. My Anorexia has been much more to the fore today, especially with body checking and just general dissatisfaction with my new, "improved" physique. Emily leaving has only added to the generally sad feeling.

Michelle says hi + that ur a legend.

Vicky

Bless you. The hardest thing was saying goodbye to you and Abbie. I'll miss you guys so much.

Emily.

CARRY ON NURSING

Poole Surgery,
Poole

22 January 2008

Dear Mr Evans

I hope you don't mind me writing to you but I passed you on your bike today and I was concerned that it appears that you've lost more weight. From a Doctor's point of view I am concerned that your anorexia may be once again an issue.

I would appreciate if you could make an appointment to see me at the Surgery to discuss this.

Yours sincerely

Dr G.P.

I was clear that Anorexia's power over me stemmed from the fact that it had given me back some of the self-esteem and sense of acceptability that I had lost through all the years of bullying and exclusion. I understood that to fully recover I needed something else to replace Anorexia as the bed rock of my self-esteem and Mental Health nursing appeared to be the perfect solution. What better and more respected position is there than working all day to save and improve lives, actually making a difference?

Kimmeridge Court had given me an idyllic vision of nursing and I was looking forward to establishing relationships with colleagues and patients, all the time buttressing my self-esteem and proving to everyone that I wasn't wasting my life away anymore. True I didn't really enjoy working on the general hospital wards, and the constant washing, walking and dressing of patients was making me very tired, but when I was a Mental Health Nurse, talking to those under my care and imparting the benefit of my own experience, everything would be fine. I convinced the University that I had my Anorexia under control and my place was secured. In preparation, I tried to get work at the hospital where I had been treated but failed to pass the Physical Intervention training required of all staff dealing with Mental Health patients. Not for the first time in my life, I was deemed not assertive enough! No matter, I wouldn't need it to be a student nurse and by the time I had qualified I would be much stronger and more confident, as I would have been four years into my miraculous, record-breaking recovery by then.

My Nurse training began in October 2007, almost two years to the day that I had been admitted to Kimmeridge Court. While I maintained a confident front to friends and family, I knew within myself that my Anorexia had returned almost as strong as ever (only almost though, I did sit down *sometimes*) but I was absolutely convinced that if I qualified as a Mental Health Nurse then my eating disorder would be consigned to history. I was also looking on this second spell at University as a chance to make up for the missed opportunity of my time in Leicester. I was determined that this time I would live the student lifestyle—as far as is possible without drinking, anyway—and make all the new friends that I failed to do nine years previously. Again, however, when there became a straight choice between my eating disorder and my new, exciting student life, there was only ever one winner.

There was a part of me that was looking forward to learning new things and testing myself in the academic world again, but Anorexia kept screaming about the long lectures and all the computer work we were expected to do or, more specifically, all the sitting down we would have to do on a routine basis, especially when we went on placement. To counteract the laziness ahead, I became even more active, using every free day and every lunch period between classes to "stretch my legs" or get some more of that fresh air that I constantly craved. Lecture days gave me the opportunity to cycle to the train station, stand up on the train throughout my journey then walk to University, where I remained upright until the last possible moment.

I still regarded myself as a breed apart, as if my childhood obesity was a sign that I was different from anyone else who had only to exercise for 30 minutes a day. I knew my weight was falling again—I was back to weighing myself on numerous occasions every day—but I had no inclination to do anything about it. I continued to see my nursing course as the solution to all my problems and felt as if all I had to do was hold it together until I qualified. I knew I couldn't cope with the guilt of resisting my Anorexia and didn't want anything to disrupt my studies, so I indulged it as much as I could and hoped for the best. I never did find the time to get to know the other students or to experience the student lifestyle—there always seemed to be something more important, or more anorexic to do.

I bluffed my way past my parents' concerns, though I did discuss my problems with my friends on the few occasions I deigned to meet up with them. It was clear by now that the dreams of recovery I had upon discharge from Kimmeridge Court had been unrealistic. Some people were able to banish their eating disorder completely from their life, but I now saw myself as facing a future in which Anorexia would continue to play a major part. And I accepted that, because I was proving that I was living and succeeding despite Anorexia's presence. I clung desperately to the fact that I was the one who hadn't gone back, "One Admission Man" who had cracked it all in three months and would never need to go back to Kimmeridge Court again. *I must never go back.*

My academic work again stood up well, and I got along ok with most of my classmates, even if never finding room in my schedule to see them outside lectures. My student placements were, however, another matter. The first, at a Day Care Centre for elderly patients, had the added complication of leaving me working alongside my Key Nurse from Kimmeridge Court! To her credit she made no mention of this and my regular cover story of having worked on the Eating Disorders Unit helped to explain our familiarity. This did mean, of course, that my activity levels were limited in her presence, so I volunteered for any errands that needed doing and continued to stand when possible. Unfortunately, I was spending so much of my day standing up or on the move that when I did sit down for any length of time, exhaustion took over and I began to fall asleep.

This became a major problem on my second placement, in May 2008, when I joined a Community Outreach Team. By this point I could no longer deny that my Anorexia had again taken over, but I felt utterly incapable of doing anything about it. I was so wedded to eating my meals four hours apart and timing each mouthful at two—or three-minute intervals that sleep had become something I fitted around the rest of my life. By the time I'd cycled the three miles to the Hospital every morning I was already yawning and looking forward to long days with only an apple to sustain myself until I got home. I was taking perverse pride in my ability to last from breakfast to tea without hardly drinking or eating anything, and I could push myself through so long as I didn't sit down. Much of the day was spent visiting patients in their homes and, once my tiredness combined with central heating, I was off. My Mentor had already admonished me for a lack of concentration and matters came to a head when I fell asleep in front of a patient whilst she was having a nervous breakdown. That was the end of the pretence—Anorexia was back and messing up my life all over again.

Later I broke down in tears and confessed all to my Mentor who, to my amazement said that she had figured out from my emaciated frame and constant standing that I might just have an eating disorder. This was absolute rock bottom. I had become so convinced that nursing was going to be my root to eternal happiness that to see myself not even capable of completing the first year of my course made it feel as if my soul had been ripped out. My academic work had continued to shine but the placements had been hard and there was no way that I would ever pass a Physical Intervention course in my current physical state. My whole motivation for starting the nursing course, aside from boosting my self-esteem, had been to use my own experiences as a "recovered" Mental Health patient to help others. With that recovery exposed as a sham, however, there was no other choice.

I quit the course, leaving my self-esteem in pieces and my Anorexia shouting from the rooftops about yet another triumph. I had little or no idea about what to do about any of it.

KIMMERIDGE COURT DIARY
WEEK 14

The week I'd been waiting for since December—target weight reached. Excited as I was about the prospect of going home a starting my "new life", this milestone also brought a whole load of fears right back to the surface, particularly about my ability to sustain the momentum and live a life in my new skin.

It helped that everyone around me offered the 100 per cent enthusiasm that I still could not quite summon up myself, as did receiving a "self-esteem card" of anonomised comments from other patients and staff. I don't care how miserable I feel, seeing that someone described me as "FAB company" is something that will always make me smile. Great idea.

Friday 19 March: Day 96

Another low day, but still able to make "right" decisions when I have to. Anorexia still holds some appeal, even just because I wouldn't have a gut, but then I can have so much more and fat is part of everyday life and is not necessarily an inevitable part of BMI 21. I need to learn to love myself, to see in me all the good things other people do and to value them instead of some never-reached perfection. I never will be perfect. I have to ignore how I feel, because feelings change and right now I have all the support I need. I look good, better than I have for so long and I don't deserve to lose this chance.

Saturday 20 March: Day 97

Today was what it is all about. Driving for an hour, getting lost for no reason, but feeling like it didn't matter. Going for a sophisticated drink—TEA for the first time ever, out of a huge cup with extra cream—and it was enjoyable. A Chinese takeaway, with mountains of rice, which was fine, with no bad after-effects and with Abbie's support too. Meeting my mate for a drink—two drinks, no diet—and listening about his life for two hours. Brilliant stuff. And you know what, I look ok. I'm no Adonis, I'm not perfect but then who is? I'm all right, I'm a nice bloke, "sociable, funny, smiles a lot". I HAVE THAT EVIDENCE. Fact is, if I hold it together, my life can only get better from here, whatever happens.

Monday 22 March: Day 99

I've got loads of ideas about what a "Recovered Me" might look like—in a library, in Australia, in a relationship, in the pub, at the cinema, back in Wales having a good time, and there seems to be a less and less compelling case to stay with Anorexia, but still the fear of failure and the impact that would have remains. I am becoming more uneasy about pushing myself further, I continue to be dissatisfied about my "tyre", but ever more concerned that to try and affect that will lead me to over-exercise again. I don't know whether to act the big I am or to ask for help. I'm getting really excited about all these new things but I don't want to blow it by getting ahead of myself. At the moment my life as an anorexic seems quite distant, but the illness is still very much there in my make-up.

Tuesday 23 March: Day 100

BMI: 21.3

Mark today down as the first day of the rest of my life! Trying to ignore another huge gain over the weekend and concentrate on the fact that BMI 21 has been achieved. Very aware though that the hard work starts now. From now on Anorexia is going to be screaming like a klaxon, trying to tempt me to revisit old habits and start cutting back, and it will take double the effort I've shown so far to keep this going. Last time I thought getting to BMI 20 gave me licence to do anything I wanted and I took my eye off the ball almost as soon as I had it under control. I have to be on message all the time and there will be moments where it all seems too much and where Anorexia calls out to me in that way it does. It's then I will have to remember the bad old times, the hundreds of reasons I have to keep going, because if I can hold on, my life will only get better. I can't deny the fact that people like me, that some people think I'm good looking and sociable and funny, so what is there for Anorexia to offer me? If only it were that simple! One day to bask in the glory, then head down.

Good day, but loads of thoughts running through my head. Can I really do this? What if my weight keeps going up? Do I need two weeks' maintenance? Can I do it? Yes I can, there is nothing to stop me except my ability or otherwise to push this through. After discharge it is me and me alone and I have to do it for me, not for Mum, Dad, Hannah, Margot, Abbie or anyone else. The things I want—a good job, a family, a relationship, Australia—none of it is possible with Anorexia and I have to keep thinking of the good things so that when the bad times come I don't look for the solution through exercise. It will take a monumental effort but it can be done, and I do believe in myself. My weight won't keep going up and if it means missing out some of my biscuits so be it. Shame though!

(*Two weeks off*) Maintenance? I don't really know, but my instinct is pointing to leaving next week. I don't feel like I am benefitting myself or anyone else by staying longer, especially with new people coming in. Someone else out there deserves the chance I've had and I don't feel I should deprive them of it any longer than necessary. My time here has again been wonderful and I will miss Abbie like mad, but I need to sort things out with Mum and Dad and going home next week seems like the thing to do.

Good stuff—MAINTENANCE. Talking to Amber, Keir and Abbie. Texts from Hannah, Lucy and Dan.

> *You star. That's great. I hope you can feel proud of yourself as I think the way you have gone about all this is amazing. I'm just glad I could be here for you. You're a great mate and I'm so proud of you.*
>
> *Hannah*

Wednesday 24 March: Day 101

Not sure where I am at the moment and how confident I am about how much is going to change. My weight and all the issues around it seem less important somehow and less of a problem. I am confident that I can find an eating/exercise balance that will allow me to maintain at BMI 21 and that that will give me the solid platform from which to go forward. I certainly believe that my problems with Mum and Dad will be solved if I can sustain my recovery and that the act of maintaining my weight will in itself boost my confidence and help me approach relationships in a more positive way. Beneath all that, though, there are so many things that remain—my cautious approach to relationships, my continued inability to value my own qualities and my failure to steer my self-esteem from how I look. Why do I think all my friends are doing me a favour? Why do I focus on possible negative outcomes? I've done so much since I've been here, challenged so much and I still feel ok, but there remains a serious nagging doubt behind my recovery. I believe I will be ok, I really do, but I can't be certain, and maybe that's my problem. If any element of doubt exists I become very reluctant to take the risk, in life, in relationships, in my diet, but if I keep safe, keep shying away from risks and chance and life I will never beat Anorexia, as the only way to escape its grasp is to challenge it.

Thursday 25 March: Day 102

BMI: 21.2

Discharge next Thursday. Excited and scared tenfold compared to what I've felt so far. All my feelings are close to the surface at the moment and keeping them in check seems a much harder task than anything to do with eating. The fact is that it is going to take a long time to get through the rubbish underpinning the eating disorder, but why would I turn to restriction/exercise as a solution to my life? If I have learnt anything this time it is surely that the solution to the world's problems does not lie in a set of scales.

I'm still really scared of starting to re-train with exercise. All evidence says that either I repeat every day or that repetitions get more frequent and take longer, with all associated knock-on effects for my social life. Like I said to Dr. Macken, I don't want a six-pack if I'm the only one who's going to see it.

REACHING ROCK BOTTOM—AGAIN

Having set so much stall by nursing as my route to happiness, I was now left with a massive void in my life. As well as my failure to complete even the first year of my course, I now had to face up to the fact that my Anorexia was back stronger than ever and any hope I still clung to of changing my behaviour now left me.

My G.P. was talking again in terms of a return to Kimmeridge Court, but my continued "success" in being a once-only inpatient was about the only thing that was keeping me going. It was now evident that my admission had done nothing to banish the unhelpful thoughts or the core beliefs underpinning my Anorexia, and I did not want to go through the cycle of physical recovery again as I saw no way in which it would not inevitably be followed by a return to old ways. I knew how much faith my parents had put in my first admission to be the thing that "cured" me, and I did not want to raise their hopes again if there was no guarantee that anything would change. I had been living with an eating disorder for twelve years and I had always had the underlying belief that one day a switch would flick on and everything would be ok. For the first time that switch appeared out of reach.

Resigned to the fact that my life was destined to be an anorexic one, I set out to ensure that I did everything I could to satisfy the illness and to lessen the immense feelings of guilt that it engendered every time I refused to obey its directions. I had continued to work at the shop on weekends and when a supervisor's role on the evening shift came up I grabbed it with both hands. The job involved seven hour shifts of heavy, manual work, all spent on foot and with plenty of opportunities to indulge my Anorexia. I was even given responsibility for staff security checks, each one of which involved a trip up and down stairs, and I made sure to respond to every call even if the security guard was close by. It has been years since I actually "enjoyed" the constant journeys up and down stairs, in the sense that I felt I was gaining something tangible by neglecting the opportunity to use the lift or escalator. It simply became something I "had" to do, like the walking and the gym and the cycling, another method with which to keep the fatness and the guilt at bay for another day.

My shift at the shop was from 3 p.m. to 10 p.m., which not only gave me plenty of daytime hours to go for walks and fit in an hour's worth of sit-ups and weight lifting, but also had the added bonus of giving me an excuse not to go out and meet friends. This allowed me to avoid any situations in which there may be a danger of having to eat or drink something, but also meant I did not have to face the questions and concerns of people becoming increasingly concerned about my physical condition.

My routine was so sacrosanct that anything that disrupted it sent me into flurries of panic and would invariably lead to a reduction in my diet. The prospect of my parents visiting still meant weeks of stress in anticipation. The only way I could even contemplate going out for a meal with them was if we walked to the only local restaurant whose entire menu and calorific content data was available online. In January 2009 I felt so sure that Anorexia would be with me forever that I sat my parents down and calmly explained how I had accepted this and that I now had to do all I could to remain sane and to stay away from death's door, which included doing a job way below my capabilities and having complete control over what I ate. I'd given up pretending that I was "ok" and that I was happy—indeed I confessed that I hadn't been happy for thirteen years—and I now just wanted to live my anorexic life alone for however long it lasted.

In the three years since my discharge from Kimmeridge Court I had lost 14 kg (the scales were again being consulted every couple of hours) and every small decrease was met with renewed determination that this time I would start fighting back. And yet the downward spiral would continue, the 450 calorie limit on meals sank to 440 and then to 430, the "head start" added on my food scales went from 5 grams to 10 and then to 20. Meals, planned with military precision, allowed only the lowest fat, lowest calorie ingredients, more and more of which went straight from plate to bin without getting anywhere near my mouth.

Every part of my body from my jaw bone to my shoulders to my backside became a checkpoint to ensure that no, that banana had not turned me into a hippo. I couldn't pass a mirror without stopping to admire my thinness or resist the occasional attempt to jump on the spot before taking perverse pleasure in my failure to do so, confirming as it did that I had pushed my body so far beyond where it is comfortable to go.

Certain things had been maintained since Kimmeridge Court. I did sit down occasionally and I was no longer eating in such a methodical, time-consuming way, but this just gave me more time to exercise. I avoided driving as much as possible as I couldn't stand being forced to sit down for such long periods, to the extent that my car battery ran down through lack of use. I had reached the very definite conclusion that to be happy I had to obey my Anorexia at every turn, and I was content that this was what my life would amount to. All the time while I indulged my Anorexia I was convincing myself that I was having the best life possible and I still hadn't had to go back to Kimmeridge Court. I had a rubbish job, no social life to speak of and had driven my parents to the point of despair, but at least I hadn't gone back.

It wasn't long before my behaviour raised questions at work. The management were blissfully unaware of any problems, but my supervisor, Keir, who had become a good mate and would later prove a great source of strength, began to pick me up on my method of work. Things that before could be written off as eccentricities—always using the stairs, going for a walk on my break, walking back and forth from shelf to stock—were now seen as a bad example to be setting by someone in a supervisory role. I tried all manner of excuses and bluffs to cover my tracks, but my actions were having an impact on the team's performance and Keir was getting grief because of it. In the grip of my Anorexia there haven't been many times of regret at the consequences of my behaviour on other people, but I really did hate the fact that I was letting him down so much, and this is where I began to realise how utterly incapable I was of changing under my own initiative. Truth was Keir and the rest of the staff kept me in a job by doing most of my work for me. At the end of each shift I rewarded myself with a quick sniff of the pick n' mix aisle, those intoxicating aromas offering a brief journey into the forbidden in much the same way as the smell of the fish and chip shop or the curry houses in Manchester had done before. It was as if I had to continually test the boundaries of my willpower, never really believing that Anorexia would one day let me taste as well as smell. With every act of resistance Anorexia got stronger, feeding off the sense of exhilaration that coursed through me every time I did what I had to do.

The things that I had been happy to do to comply with my Anorexia—the weighing, the checking, the constant, endless exercise—began to become more onerous and, when I finally agreed to meet Hannah, my best friend, after months of avoiding her, her reaction to my emaciated frame did much to shake me out of my delusion. I continued on the treadmill of my life, still indulging my Anorexia at every turn, still meeting every fall in weight with renewed determination to change before excoriating myself for losing the enthusiasm so quickly. Eventually, my G.P.'s suggestions about a return to Kimmeridge Court began to hit home. In the run-up to Christmas work in the shop was extremely hectic, meaning longer hours and even more opportunity to exercise and avoid eating. I was back to wearing three layers, cycling to work in the wind and the rain and covering the numerous cuts on my hands and feet in plasters so that I could continue working. Something in me realised quite how sorry my life had become.

I really had convinced myself that, if I gave up fighting and gave up any hope of living life without Anorexia, then things would be easier. By always hoping and waiting for things to change I had clung onto the anger I felt towards myself for being incapable of beating it. By offering no resistance to Anorexia's call I was sure that it would make life easier, and I tried, I really did try to give up fighting and to let Anorexia win. Nothing changed. My life did not get any easier, the thoughts never eased off and my days were just as empty and guilt-ridden as they had always been. I had finally given my illness everything it asked for and still the voice just would not stop. And now, after years of trying to keep Anorexia at bay, I could no longer hold back the tiny bit of "John" that had remained.

Increasingly, the prospect of a shameful return to Kimmeridge Court did not appear quite so bad given the alternative of my current situation, and I had a sense that I deserved one more shot at life. I asked my G.P. to refer me back to the Eating Disorders Service, conscious that if this had any chance of working I had to tackle this head-on and in a different way to four years previously. First decisions: a change of therapist and choosing not to jog to my first appointment!

I went into that first meeting completely dead set against inpatient treatment, and explained my reasons behind this, but as he went through the options, including a place on the service's new non-residential unit, I began to see that in reality there really was no option. I hadn't expected him to suggest an inpatient admission—as usual I had underestimated quite how desperate my situation had become—but as I sat there the prospect of taking a break from my life became more and more appealing. True, I would no longer be able to claim that I had been "cured" after one admission, and the prospect of "Stretch and Relax" classes and the dreaded Fortisip drink filled me with foreboding, but I again began to feel a sense of relief in admitting that my life had descended backwards into my Anorexia and in having had the strength to share this with someone else.

I left convinced that I needed to go back as an inpatient, determined to learn from my first admission and to make sure this really was the last time. Just six months previously I had openly accepted that my life would be an anorexic one forever, and that to be happy I would have to live alongside my illness and obey it at every turn. It was becoming obvious, though, that happiness would never be an option and the small part of me that remained "John" was not willing to settle for the compromised life I had been living.

Only my sister knew of my decision to refer myself back into the care of Kimmeridge Court and I only told my parents the day before I was to be readmitted to the inpatient unit. I didn't want to raise their hopes again, especially when I was undecided as to how I wanted to take this forward, but mostly I wanted to do this alone as I saw it as part of the growing up that would be vital if I was to finally start to fight back. My over-reliance on my parents, even years after I had left home, had kept me clinging to certain aspects of my childhood and would never allow me to move on to a life beyond Anorexia.

My parents were pleased though I could sense their scepticism that things would change, and to be honest I was unsure myself, but I had run out of answers. My work were fantastic in giving me as much time off as I needed and I entered Kimmeridge Court for the second time just under four years since my discharge from my first admission. For everything I'd done and achieved in that period, I was back at the very bottom, but something did feel different. I knew how big a decision it had been to swallow my pride and to return, and making that move meant all bets were off. It felt like there was one less barrier to what I could now achieve.

My life to this point had been about being the best, at school, at football knowledge, at being thin and then at recovering from Anorexia. I had to accept second best, to realise that merely staying away from Kimmeridge Court did not constitute recovery from Anorexia and learn to be happy in the knowledge that though there would always be someone "better" than me, that all I could do would be to be the best "John" that I could be. Anorexia had been my support for fourteen years and, whilst I had always wanted to break away, I had never been able to sustain the effort required for long enough. I still held that determination, I had the support of Kimmeridge Court behind me and I had no other answers left.

11 December 2009

Dear Dr G.P.

   Thank you for referring John to the Eating Disorders Service. John has now completed two appointments with myself to assess his present situation and how to proceed from here.
   As you are aware John presents with an extensive loss of weight down to approximately a BMI of 15.7. His true BMI is probably slightly less than this as this reflects his weight clothed. He continues to eat a reasonable amount of food however John's main concern is the level of compulsive exercise he engages in, as a result of the amount of food he eats. Unless he completes a certain level of activity he cannot eat as much. John reports feeling physically weak and tired constantly and has some concerns as regards to his ability to continue to do his job. His present job was secured on the basis of the level of activity that was expected of him.
   Overall it is clear that John is suffering from a relapse of his eating disorder and this resembles a typically anorexia nervosa presentation with a particular focus on compulsive exercise as the main manifestation. John describes very limited social activity outside of work. This is hampered as much by the demands of his eating disorder as it is by the limited range of friends and acquaintances that he has. He is also using hand creams for difficulties and problems with his hands. We discussed the various options for treatment and as we did so it became clear that the single most appropriate one was inpatient treatment. This is because John did not feel he would be able to break the pattern at home at the present time and that the extra support available on the inpatient unit would help him to do so.
   Should you have any queries about this letter, please do not hesitate to contact me.

Yours sincerely

Dr M.H. Therapist

KIMMERIDGE COURT DIARY
WEEK 15

My final week as an inpatient and, in many ways, it felt like the last four months had never happened. Now I had reached my target and I wasn't focused on gaining weight, all the familiar guilty feelings around food and exercise were once again plaguing my thoughts and really causing me to doubt whether I could pull this off. For the first time in years I genuinely had some fat on my body and I was struggling to deal with this fact.

And yet something was different, the good words were still getting through and, bizarrely, I was still enjoying being around people and friends and not going for a run instead. I was certainly more fearful than following my first admission, when I could see nothing holding me back from the life I wanted to lead, but I also felt more excited, more open to a path other to that down which Anorexia wanted me to go. I knew how hard the future would be, but I sensed that that future was in my hands.

Friday 26 March: Day 103

A really mixed day when the struggle ahead of me seemed more mountainous than ever, but I have also been given even more reason to keep going. There is no doubt that the anorexic voice is getting stronger the more I revisit old territory and begin to adapt to my new reality. On Thursday I will leave the place I've been happiest these last fourteen years (*Kimmeridge Court*) and crash straight back into my lonely, screwed-up life, where the fear remains that one critical comment could send me backwards.

Saturday 27 March: Day 104

Another really testing day where the urge to check myself and to reassure myself that all is well was almost overwhelming. I always knew this would be hard and that the real work would begin with maintenance, and that is becoming very apparent. I'm not sure if the doubts came back so quickly last time (*first admission*), but maybe it's because I'm aware of previous "failures". What seems so easy at Kimmeridge Court seems thousands of times harder at home, but then I suppose that's why I have to get out of there and back to the real world. Somehow I have to transfer the good vibes and carry them with me, begin to believe the positive things I am being told about how I am and how I look. There is still a very real danger that Anorexia will smack itself right back into my life unless I find other, more important things, upon which to hang my self-esteem.

There are so many good reasons to recover—work, Hannah, Abbie among them—but still that is not enough. Fundamentally it comes down to whether I want my anorexic life or if I want a better life. By rejecting my Anorexia I take on the pain and the anxiety that goes with that decision, the increasingly loud and increasingly frequent anorexic voice beckoning me back to his arms every time a choice has to be made. By looking for something—anything—better I have to take the risk that there is nothing better, that I was right all along and that I will be a blimp. I remain petrified at the thought of being overweight and I just hope my work with Dr. Macken can help eradicate this. But do I want Anorexia in my life? No. Decision made.

Sunday 28 March: Day 105

Yet more evidence today of the rubbish that Anorexia brings with it. Sitting with Margot today was like talking to myself five months ago—taking long routes, over-exercising, under-eating, almost feeling as if there is no escape—and I find myself incapable of giving her any better advice than I was able to give myself. I can't be hypocritical and say she shouldn't go out or she must eat because I have done exactly those things and more and had that same feeling that I was different to everyone else, somehow special.

I'm still scared that I am headed for an almighty fall, that despite my confidence and belief all this will be for nothing.

Monday 29 March: Day 106

Interesting question in Self Esteem Group today—how have I begun to accept compliments and use them to counter my core beliefs? I think it comes down to my ability to step outside of my Anorexia here, to be confident enough to be myself. All the compliments, and there have been quite a few, are for me as a person, not as a pupil or worker. I have begun to recognise the huge controlling influence Anorexia has had on my life and therefore the hugely detrimental impact it has had on my ability to be an effective worker, family member and friend. I can't deny that I've made mistakes, caused Mum, Dad and my sister worry or that I've neglected my friends, and I may find that Anorexia was not responsible for this, but I know my life could have been so different if it hadn't darkened my door.

Ah well, shit happens.

Tuesday 30 March: Day 107

BMI: 21.4

Up ½ kg today, and though I don't really feel any different, it's amazing how knowing I am heavier makes me focus on my waistline—always my waistline. Looking at myself in my new clothes I can see that I look much better, but it remains difficult to look beyond the "tyre". Getting increasingly worried about going back to work. My self-esteem is too fragile at the moment to cope with any verbal attacks. What if my poor performance was not Anorexia's fault?

Wednesday 31 March: Day 108

Relationship Group was actually really useful today. I have spent the last fourteen years getting angry—with myself, my situation, my failures, my parents for not accepting my Anorexia. I feel as if I have finally tried to turn that around, becoming angry with rather than about my Anorexia and realising that if I am to move on then I have to leave it all—resentment, eating disorder, everything—all in the past. If I try to convince my parents that I have changed, I am barking up the wrong tree. I don't really expect them to believe me—why should they?—and becoming frustrated with them for not believing me will only serve to reignite the anger that I am trying to shed. Our relationship does need to change: I need to be an equal partner in the relationship, as with all other relationships, and I need to find something other than their approval (whether I believe it or not) on which to base my self-esteem.

I am still scared that all this will be for nothing, that as soon as my ego stops being massaged then I will fall back, but something has changed, I believe that and I think the only person I really need to convince is myself. None of it lessens the hard work ahead or the very real fears I have, but at least I now have hope.

Thursday 1 April: Final Day

Time to go. I feel really empty, as if I'm leaving my new life behind again and going into the unknown. I think—*I believe*—that I can carry this through but there are so many questions to which I don't know the answer—what do I do about the first setback? What if Hannah moves away? Will I be able to drag things back if it happens again? Can I find something other than my parents' approval on which to base my life? I am excited by the possibilities, but there is little happiness in leaving today. Why would there be—this has been a four month ego trip! What I have to do is push this through to the real world, to give them the version of John that has emerged and flourished these past few months. I have enough qualities—intellectually, personally, practically—to live the life I want but it is up to me. Scary!

Today has reiterated what all this has been about. I feel like I have so much more to lose this time, least of all my pride. The strength that everyone on the unit has shown and the fact that they believe I have in some way inspired them gives me a boost that I haven't really felt for a long time. There are so many people above and beyond my family who care for me that I can't rely on my waistline for my happiness any more. I am worth more. To new beginnings.

> *Hey you. Good luck for 2day, everything will be ok. If anyone can do it you can x.*
>
> *Emily*

> *. . . . just wanted to let you know ur missed enormously already but the units loss is the big wide worlds gain*
>
> *Suzie*

Thank you for the words you wrote to me, they mean so much. I feel that you are a true friend for life, for the ups and the downs. Congrats again on reaching freedom. I hope it will set you free to be the wonderful person I know you are in every sense.

Hannah.

SELF-ESTEEM

I JUST GOT YOUR CARD,
THANK YOU FOR WHAT YOU
WROTE—THAT MEANS SO
MUCH TO ME. I HAVE ALWAYS
FELT THAT YOU HAVE BEEN
THERE FOR ME TOO—YOUR
VISITS WHEN I DID MY SECOND
KIM STINT WERE WHAT KEPT
ME SANE. I AM SO GLAD YOU
DECIDED TO GO BACK AND
IT MAKES ME REALLY REALLY
HAPPY TO HAVE "JOHN" BACK.
I HOPE THAT YOU WILL BE A
FRIEND FOR LIFE
HANNAH

KIMMERIDGE COURT
OUTPATIENT DIARY

Friday 2 April

Back in Wales and suddenly things seem so much tougher. For fourteen years my life here has been intertwined with my Anorexia and the way it has come between myself, my family and my friends. I refused extra helpings earlier, even before my brain had processed the thought and it's almost as if my Anorexia is finding it easier to impose itself in this place where it has always been so strong. My instinct remains an anorexic one: *that banana is too big; I have to stand; I have to go for a walk;* and while I can presently rationalise these thoughts, the memories of my previous "recovery" are painfully clear in my mind. It was good, though, to catch up with Dan. Hopefully one day I will have what he has.

Saturday 3 April

Just a really good day. Warning signs and bad feelings remain—about my body shape, about my relationship with my parents, about how much is "enough"—but I broke so many rules today that I can't help but be positive. All that sitting down, choosing the car over walking, asking for biscuit cake, breaking the four hour rule to fit into my social life, two drinks—each is one more V sign to Anorexia. Also great to be with friends who remember "John", before Anorexia replaced them in my life and who stuck by me regardless of the selfish shell that I became.

Sunday 4 April

The more time I spend in Wales now the more I realise that, whatever the future holds, I have to make my life away from here. Physically I moved away a long time ago, but mentally I don't think I ever truly have, always clinging to the hope that I could come back and everything would be like 1998 again. But that past has gone, everyone has moved on and it's time I did so too.

This weekend has gone as well as I could have hoped and has only reinforced my desire to beat this, whilst again highlighting how tough it will be. Almost every decision I make day-to-day has an anorexic twist to it and having to make the "right" decision every time is a daunting prospect. But the reaction of everyone, Mum, Dad, my sister, most importantly Dan, Rob and Sam, has given me a glimpse of how life could be without Anorexia and how people react to me differently just because I look well. I have to hold onto that, whatever life throws at me. PMA son, PMA.

Tuesday 6 April

My first day on the outpatient unit at Kimmeridge and many old fears remain. I'm still finding it difficult to accept my body as it is. Fat has been such a no-no for so long that to feel its presence on my body still seems tremendously uncomfortable. I just have to remember that *everybody* who matters—Hannah, Mum, Dad, my sister, Abbie—prefer me as I am now. I will get used to it. I have to believe that. I have no other answers.

Wednesday 7 April

Overall picture remains good and for the first time in years I am happy, actually genuinely happy and looking forward to the future. The major thing is the reaction I'm getting, especially from Hannah but also Mum, Dad, Abbie, Dan, Rob and everyone else who smiles now when they see me. I've spent so many years believing that I have to be thin to be likeable, but it appears as though I have to be healthy to be liked, or at least that people like me more when I'm healthy. I despise Anorexia and all the heartache it has caused me, but if I had never gone through this then I would never have met some of the most important people in my life, and I would not be the man I am today. And I like the man I am today.

Thursday 8 April

The shit really is beginning to hit the fan now. I KNOW I'm not fat and I know that my life now is 2000% better, but it still does not stop me hating the fact that I now have fat on my body and I can't stop focusing on it. Everything is so positive most of the time but it only takes some indigestion or a large meal to bring Anorexia right back into play. I do believe this will right itself in time. I hope I am right.

Monday 12 April

Again just a day full of good stuff and good reasons to keep going but which ends with my feeling dissatisfied with my stomach. It is so hard to get used to my body and I'm beginning to imagine growth where realistically there is none. I have learnt to value my other qualities and all the positive feedback about my new clothes, my new look, me as a person, all of it makes me feel ten feet tall, but when I'm alone, I find it hard not to focus on what I have feared for so long.

Thursday 15 April

First swimming lesson today—proper fear-confronting stuff that! Swimming is something I've avoided purely out of fear, not of the water or of drowning or even so that people wouldn't see me half naked. It has been solely because of my fear of being seen to be a failure and being laughed at for not being able to swim. And that is why I have to do it and why I have to talk at the Kimmeridge Court workshop (*on Eating Disorders*) tomorrow. Anorexia is screaming at me not to bother, because I will be made to look a fool and because people will laugh at me. If I don't do it then Anorexia will win again.

Friday 16 April

Thank you so much John for your contribution to the workshop. I hope you could tell from what people said how valuable they found hearing from you . . . . I hope you have a good weekend and are able to bask a little in your achievement.

Dr D.R.

Monday 19 April

In "Self-Esteem Group" today we were asked to make a list of self-critical thoughts personal to us. In the past I have had no problem coming up with a whole list but today I really struggled. At the moment I am happy with who I am and how I am living my life in accordance with the values that I hold dear to me presently. I am a good friend, I am honest and clever and increasingly confident and the only thing that really causes me to doubt myself is my recovery and my ability to stick things out. Last time I "recovered" I had these same doubts but did not acknowledge them and they just built up and built up until I couldn't and didn't want to do anything about them. I hope this time will be different.

Tuesday 20 April

What I should have said in the workshop last Friday was that I am no longer angry with the Anorexia for cocking up my life, what's done is done. I am no longer angry with my parents for trying to come between me and my Anorexia. And I am no longer angry with myself. None of this is my fault, but it is the hand that life has dealt me. To accept that and to fight my way back is, I reckon, a pretty good thing to aim for and to be known for. Life *will* be good.

Wednesday 28 April

My last day as a Kimmeridge Court outpatient and, therefore, the last of these entries. I haven't written anything for the past couple of days because the message was becoming very repetitive. Recovery is as hard, if not harder than I expected, but I have not experienced any deterioration in my central belief—I can and will beat this illness. When I think back five months to the scared, beaten individual who began this journey, I find myself incapable of tuning in to how he felt or thought, other than knowing that the progress I have made would have seemed impossible at that time. Had I known and believed then what I know and believe about myself now then I would never have resisted my return to Kimmeridge Court for so long. As well as not wanting to give up my Anorexia, I thought my return would confirm my failure to recover after my first admission, and I could see no way in which the experience could match up. How wrong I was!

By accepting defeat in my personal struggle and asking for help, I was able to focus all my effort and (limited) strength on fighting my one, greatest enemy. I was able to take on new challenges and to build up the confidence to enable me to change routines and habits that had become ingrained over fourteen years. I was allowed to see that I had been wrong, that there was a way out for me as there is for anybody who has the will, the support and the belief in themselves. Again that support—from the Kimmeridge Court staff and the best bunch of fellow patients I could have hoped for—was immense and enabled me to see a better, more confident, happier version of "John" than the anorexic that had drifted through life since University. I had become so lost, so immersed in my Anorexia that I needed help to pull away and to see that life without an eating disorder was possible. Whatever kind of man I am today is due in no small part to the people I have encountered on this journey.

And that, I think, is the point—I am now a man. For so many years I have shied away from life, kept my Anorexia close so as to protect myself from "adult" situations—jobs, socialising, relationships—so that I could cling to a happier time, before the bullying and the sadness and the insecurity. Being a man seemed so responsible, so risky, so potentially dangerous that it appeared safer to say and do nothing that would expose me, and this gave Anorexia the perfect environment in which to thrive. Only now do I feel confident to put "John" out there, because only now do I feel confident in the fact that "John" is someone people like and feel comfortable to be around. There are only so many times you can be described as an "inspiration" and continue to ignore it! I now feel ready to step out from behind my parents, to step away from the eight-year-old boy that I have looked back at so longingly and to take my place as a fully paid up member of society, whatever excitements, disappointments and risks that might hold.

And my Anorexia? Still a long way to go, still something that keeps one finger of its grip on my shoulder. I remain petrified of being overweight and remain uneasy about my BMI 22 body. I accept that the image I see is different to that seen by other people and that I AM NOT FAT. I hope in time that I will get used to and accept my body in its current shape, but most of all I hope that one day I will forget what it feels like to care about my body, about how it was the only important thing in life to reach the end of the day without having put on weight and how everything in the world was fine as long as I'd had "enough" exercise. Anorexia doesn't allow for "enough", no limit is permanent or insurmountable and it will keep on pushing and pushing and pushing until you either give up fighting and ask for help or you die. Asking for help has saved my life both physically and spiritually, on more than one occasion. Do I have it in me to keep fighting, to keep drawing on the support that I need to beat this and to avoid sinking back into Anorexia's arms as I have always done before?

PMA.
Forward not back.
I BELIEVE.

NO FUTURE IN THE PAST

20 January 2011

Dear Dr G.P.

  I met with John on 20 January to close his treatment with the Eating Disorders Service.

  John's weight is 63 kg, giving him a BMI of 21.1, just inside the healthy weight range. John reports feeling much better in himself and he describes no eating disorder behaviours. There are eating disorder thoughts present, however these are very minimal and since his discharge in April there has been continued reduction in his concern with shape and weight. . . . . John continues to socialise with his network of friends both from his current work place and from people he has met whilst in treatment for his eating disorder. John describes himself as being happy and is determined to continue to maintain the progress he has made.

  Overall then John has done extremely well and completed a lot of work to establish his recovery and maintain it now for 10 months post discharge from inpatient care. I believe the risks are low in all areas for John given the stability of his recovery, his employment, his stable accommodation and his social network. John and I agreed to his discharge from the service as of today, we said our goodbyes and John also said his farewells to other members of the team.

Yours Sincerely
Dr M.H. Therapist

Thursday 28 April 2011

The night after I got the e-mail I couldn't sleep. Finally, after all the rejections and the nice words about how my story was "interesting but unfortunately not for us", finally I was being the offered the chance to get my story into print. I had the buzz again, where a hundred and one ideas and possibilities hurtle round your brain and whilst you're trying to contain the euphoria—because you know it could all go wrong—you just can't help smiling at the prospect of it all going spectacularly right. It's a feeling that I've felt more than once in the past year, and it's a feeling that surpasses anything Anorexia ever offered me. Anorexia made me safe, secure, superior, acceptable, but it never sent adrenaline rushing through my whole body so fast I wasn't sure whether I could keep it in.

The dreams I had a year ago when I left Kimmeridge Court have been more than fulfilled, the doubts I held still remain to some extent, but they have been reduced and I believe they will continue to disappear as my recovery proceeds. I made it to Australia for Christmas, I've learnt to swim, I've been for more coffees with more friends than I could have possibly imagined and, three months ago, I was discharged as a Mental Health outpatient. When I think back to the really dark times, to when "Anorexic John" was so consumed by the illness that barely a trace of my own soul existed, there was no way I'd have gone half a day without stepping gingerly onto the scales, let alone a whole year (and counting). It would have been inconceivable to meet a friend if there was exercise to be done, or to have drunk anything other than mineral water if I had managed to find a gap in my schedule. I'd never have considered Australia, because I couldn't have sat down on the plane for 24 hours and I couldn't have risked exposing my body to all the surfers on the beach for them to ridicule me. I wouldn't, to my mind, have deserved to spend that much money on myself. In the past year, when the determination and the excitement and the PMA has started to wane a little, I have never once contemplated a return to Anorexia.

Finally I feel as if my past can be left where it is, back when I didn't know what I was capable of and when I could see no other solutions to the problems in my life. I recognise now, more than ever, that my eating disorder cannot provide me with the life I want. "Divorce" is not enough for me anymore. I've seen enough over the past year, in other people and in myself, to see that a complete recovery is possible and that it is possible for me. I know there is still more of John to come out and, though there have been difficult moments since I left Kimmeridge Court, nothing has ever tempted me to go back. When I left Kimmeridge Court the first time, I basked in the glory of being physically fit. I had so many people saying I looked good and was so thrilled at the prospect of being able to do proper exercise that I was able to ignore my complete failure to tackle the underlying issues behind my eating disorder. Discharge number two was different. Yes, the comments about my appearance were still there, and I loved the opportunity to revamp my wardrobe and start swimming, but what had far greater impact were the things that told me that I had changed as a person. The way old friends reacted around me and smiled at me and told me they couldn't believe I was the same person meant more to me than a thousand words about how good I was looking.

I can see that I look good, better than I've ever looked before, and yet the fact that I remain unsatisfied with my body is the clearest indication that Anorexia is still there, waiting for the opportunity to seduce me again. Even now my mood and my outlook on my recovery can fluctuate greatly. Today, as I write, I feel good, optimistic about the future. Today I am John the author, John the friend, John the future qualified librarian. Last month I felt stuck, frustrated that even though I have lived in this body for a year I still haven't come to terms with it. After fourteen years living in suspended animation, it has sometimes been unsettling coming into contact with my emotions, at the same time experiencing life as a "normal" member of society, with no barrier in people's eyes to what I can now achieve. Sometimes I feel like I still need the recognition and the security of being "John the Anorexic". Sometimes the thought of going back to BMI 20 and the lowest edge of "healthy" presents itself as the solution to the doubts I have about my body, but the risk of descending again into Anorexia remains too high for me to even look in that direction.

Anorexia reminds me every day of its presence, not just in the pills I take for my osteoporosis but whenever I look in the mirror or feel ill or let negative thoughts enter my head it's there, offering me a way out. When I'm happy, when I'm with friends, when I'm at work it cannot touch me, because those moments provide me with more than Anorexia ever could, but still there are times when the constant battling seems too difficult to sustain and the taunts return: *fat, ugly, worthless, blimp*. My Anorexia's had a brilliant time with this book, telling me at every turn that it's boring, that no-one will read it and that the people who have said it was worth doing were only being polite, but then that just tells me that by even finishing my story I have scored another huge victory. The thought of being reviewed, of having my work assessed as a true account of the illness I've lived with for half my life fills me with dread, but again it is a risk I have to take, and another step on the road to accepting that perfection is unrealistic.

And Anorexia continues to haunt the lives of the people I love, those who have shared my journey and have done so much to show me that there is more to John than an eating disorder. I would dearly love to help them in the way they helped me but, as my parents discovered when confronted with my Anorexia, I find myself utterly incapable of offering anything other than words. I hope that by living my life as best I can away from the restrictions that Anorexia imposed upon me, I can show that there is hope for everyone, but I know better than anyone that the fight has to come from within. And every time I see someone I care about struggling, it makes me more and more angry with Anorexia, an anger that is deeper and more intense than anything I ever summoned up when consumed in my own illness. And I am even more impotent now than I was then, because Anorexia cannot be shouted out or pulled out or beaten in any way unless the person at the centre wishes it to be so.

So all I can do is keep fighting my own battle, to do all I can to expunge Anorexia from my life so that one day I can offer something more to those who are suffering as I have done. I still have those moments of doubt, snapshots of anxiety in which I have to touch my body to check it isn't expanding or read over the letters and text messages to confirm that, yes, they really did call me an "inspiration". Regrets still arise, especially when I see pictures of my friends from University getting together. I sometimes think that if it hadn't been for Anorexia then I would have been invited too, but other than that I have come to accept the hand I have been dealt. I would never have chosen to live my life as I have but what's happened has happened and it's led me to the life I have now of which I have few complaints.

Without taking the path I have I would never have met the friends I now hold dearest to my heart nor become the man I am today. Amidst the bullying and the sadness and the isolation brought on by Anorexia I seriously doubted whether John could ever be acceptable, but John has turned out to be ok. I like the way he can change his plans, exercise and all, to go for a drink with a friend. I like the way he swears too much and spends way too much money on CDs he never listens to. I like the way that he knows he's not perfect, and the way that being perfect no longer seems quite as important as it used to be. I like the way that I look better than I ever have done before. I like the way in which I can now talk of John without putting him in quotation marks, because John is real now, warts and all. There is no doubt that Anorexia is still there waiting for me but even so, there have been countless occasions over the last year when I would quite happily have accepted my recovery stopping where it is now. I am genuinely happy in a way that surpasses anything "Anorexic John" ever experienced and, had I been offered this life a year ago, I would have accepted it like a shot.

There is more to come, however, more of John to present to the world and more about myself that I have to discover. I don't feel like settling for 80% happiness any more. And so I keep fighting, trying to keep on making the right decisions every day until, I believe, those decisions will no longer offer an "anorexic option". If nothing else, starting on the road to recovery has given me a choice, not just to do the things of which my healthy body is now capable, but also the choice not to do those things even when Anorexia is screaming at me to push as far as I can. I have seen enough in myself in the last year to know that I will win this battle, and telling my story to anyone who will listen is just another step in the process. If you have been able to take something from this account of my relationship with Anorexia, whether you are a healthcare professional, a carer, a sufferer or, as I was at the start of this journey, you've just been wondering what those silly thin girls are thinking, then that makes this whole endeavour even more worthwhile. If there is one person who passes this book to someone they know and can say, "Read this, this is what I'm talking about", then I will really have achieved something.

If you are a man who finds any of this ringing true, I hope you find the strength within yourself to seek help, because believe me it takes a brave person to admit that they can't keep fighting alone. I can't promise that you'll be as lucky as I was in terms of the treatment you'll receive or the people you'll meet along the way, but someone will listen to you and offer the hand of support that is vital if Anorexia is to be beaten. Being anorexic is not a matter for shame and embarrassment, and it's not my fault or your fault or the fault of anyone who finds themselves enveloped in its shadow. And it can be beaten, however long it takes and however much support you need.

Keep believing.

CONTACTS

Beat (www.b-eat.co.uk)
The UK's largest Eating Disorders Charity
    Helpline: 0845 634 1414
    E-mail: *help@b-eat.co.uk*

I-Eat (www.i-eat.org.uk)
Support and Advice for sufferers and carers in Bournemouth
    Office open Tuesdays & Thursdays
    Contact: 07590 378822
    E-mail: *office@i-eat.org.uk.*

Men Get Eating Disorders Too (www.mengetedstoo.co.uk)
    Charitable organisation offering advice and raising awareness of eating
        disorders in men.
    E-mail: *sam@mengetedstoo.co.uk*